Foundations
of Faith

INVITED TO BELIEVE

Student Workbook 1

Wheaton Press
Train. Equip. Reflect.

Foundations of Faith
Student Workbook 1

FOR OUR CHILDREN.

THESE ARE WRITTEN THAT YOU MIGHT BELIEVE

John 20:31, NIV

Foundations of Faith

INVITED TO BELIEVE

Equipping Students to Reflect Christ

	YEAR ONE	YEAR TWO	YEAR THREE	YEAR FOUR
Growth Emphasis	An Emphasis on Believing	An Emphasis on Following	An Emphasis on Loving	An Emphasis on Going
Essential Questions	1. What does a healthy, mature follower of Christ believe? 2. How does a healthy, mature follower of Christ live?	3. How do I grow as a healthy, mature follower of Christ? 4. How do I equip others to grow as healthy, mature followers of Christ?	5. Who do others say Jesus is? 6. Who do I say Jesus is?	7. What do I believe? 8. Why do I believe? 9. How will I communicate to others?
Essential Outcomes	Understand and articulate Christ-centered beliefs	Develop authentic Christ-centered values	Develop and articulate a Christ-centered vision	Develop a clear Christ-centered personal mission
Courses	Foundations of Faith	Spiritual Formations Leadership, Evangelism, & Discipleship	Life of Christ Philosophy & Theology	Doctrine & Apologetics Christ & Culture

Class Overview

Course Essential Questions

1. What does a healthy, mature, Christ-centered theist believe?

2. How does a healthy, mature, Christ-centered theist live?

Unit Essential Questions

1. What is faith?

2. What is real?

3. What is true?

4. What is the purpose of life?

5. Is the Bible true?

6. What do I trust?

Course Description

This class will focus on inviting students to build a solid foundation of belief in the person of Christ and His teachings. Students will examine the Christ-centered theistic worldview in comparison to other major worldviews and will gain an understanding of what it means to apply God's invitation to love Him with all of their hearts, souls, and minds. Students will be challenged to apply the definitions of faith and truth in their examination of the claim of the Bible as God's collected book of inerrant revelation. Ultimately, the course will provide the opportunity to gain an understanding of the whole of Scripture in view of the mission of God.

Learning Outcomes

A. Understand and apply the basic concept of epistemology as it relates to the understanding of faith and truth

B. Identify the basic elements of a worldview and articulate the differences between materialism, idealism, dualism, and theism

C. Examine the foundational elements of faith systems and understand the foundational distinctions of a Christ-centered worldview

D. Examine the distinctly Christian belief that truth is not subjective but defined objectively through the person of Christ (John 14:6)

E. Learn to integrate and communicate truth in the context of healthy peer dialogue (Heb. 3:13)

F. Examine evidence for Christ-centered beliefs and make individual determinations regarding reliability and trustworthiness

G. Examine historical and archeological evidence to determine whether the Bible can be trusted as the personal revelation of God

H. Develop and implement a basic apologetic for the reliability of personal belief

Unit 1   What is faith?

1.   What is the learning goal for Foundations of Faith?

2.   Why do foundations matter?

3.   What is faith, and what are the foundations of my faith?

4.   What are my personal goals for learning?

5.   Why start with worldview?

Unit 2   What is real?

1.   What is real?

2.   What are the foundational perspectives on reality?

3.   What are the faith foundations of an authentic materialist?

4.   What are the faith foundations of a pure idealist?

5.   What are the faith foundations of a complete monist?

6.   What are the faith foundations of a true theist?

7.   What are the faith foundations of a Christ-centered theist?

8.   How does worldview impact my daily life?

9.   Review: What have I learned?

10.   Assessment: How will I demonstrate learning?

11.   Assessment Review: What do I still need to learn?

Unit 3   What is true?

1. What is true, and what makes something true?

2. Can truth be objectively established, and does a standard for truth exist?

3. What is perfect, and who defines perfection?

4. What is morality, and who defines morality?

5. What is the law of noncontradiction, and how does it apply to the concept of truth?

6. Can the existence of an absolute standard be proven?

7. What are the arguments for the existence of God?

8. What do Christ-centered theists believe about the origin of truth?

9. What are two different approaches to understanding God's written revelation?

10. Review: What have I learned?

11. Assessment: How will I demonstrate what I have learned?

12. Assessment review: What do I still need to learn?

Unit 4   What are the foundations of Christ-centered faith?

1. What is the difference between a discussion and a dialogue?

2. What is man, and why are we here?

3. What is moral, why do people die, and what happens at death?

4. What is the standard for perfection?

5. Why did Jesus die?

6. What is the fullness of Christ, and how does it apply to my everyday life?

7. Review: What have I learned?

8. Assessment: How will I communicate what I have learned?

Unit 5   Is the Bible true?

1. Is the Bible worthy of our trust?

2. Where did the Bible come from, and what makes it a unique book?

3. Can we trust what was originally written?

4. What role did the scribes play in textual reliability?

5. The Shema project

6. Can we trust that we have the right books in the canon?

7. Are modern translations trustworthy?

8. Does the Bible have errors?

9. Is the Bible historically and geographically trustworthy?

10. How does archeology help us trust the reliability of the Bible?

11. The Archeology project

12. Is the Bible prophetically trustworthy?

13. Why do I choose to believe the Bible?

14. Review: What have I learned?

15. Assessment: How will I demonstrate what I have learned?

16. Assessment review: What do I still need to learn?

Final   What do I trust?

	Option A. Final exam	Option B. Presentation	Option C. Combination
1.	Review Unit 1	Assign presentations	Assign final assessments
2.	Review Unit 2	Student workday	Student workday
3.	Review Unit 3	Presentations	Presentations
4.	Review Unit 4	Presentations	Presentations
5.	Review Unit 5	Presentations	Presentations
6.	Self-assessments Cloud of Witnesses video	Self-assessments Cloud of Witnesses video	Review guide due Self-assessments
7.	Final exam	No final exam	Final exam

What is faith?

Foundations of Faith

Unit Essential Questions

1. What is the difference between faith and fantasy?

2. Why do foundations of faith matter?

Unit Learning Objectives

A. To understand the essential questions, learning objectives, and expectations for this class

B. To identify my personal learning needs

C. To develop a personalized learning plan for this class

D. To understand the difference between faith and fantasy

Unit Learning Assessments

1. "My Expectations" personal reflection handout

2. The Global Student Assessment

3. Final exam pre-assessment

4. Personal spiritual formation assessment

Essential Questions

1. What is the learning goal for Foundations of Faith?

2. Why do foundations matter?

3. What is faith, and what are the foundations of my faith?

4. What are my personal goals for learning?

5. Why start with worldview?

My Expectations

1. The name I like to be called is (nickname) _____.

2. The reason I'm taking this class (other than "because it's required") is:

3. One thing I'm looking forward to in this class is:

4. Two things I want to learn in this class include:

   1.

   2.

5. One goal I have for myself this year is:

6. One thing my teacher could pray for me about this semester would be:

7. My relationship with Jesus up to this point in my life could best be described as:

What is the difference between faith and fantasy?

A student anywhere in the world with access to the Internet needs to only look up the word "faith," as defined by the latest version of the Oxford Dictionary, to learn that the foundations of faith are under attack.

According to the Oxford Dictionary, "faith" is defined as:

> "Strong belief in the doctrines of a religion, based on spiritual conviction rather than proof."[1]

> So according to the Oxford Dictionary, faith is now the equivalent of fantasy.

Lawrence Krauss, from the University of Arizona, and other leading voices who believe in the nonexistence of a supernatural realm go so far as to not only equate faith with fantasy but to correlate facts with science.

In other words, science, which by definition means "to know," is the result of knowledge, meaning proof or facts. Faith, however, is the result of a lack of proof or facts. Faith is what we have "when we don't know."

> Reflection: What are the implications if the new Oxford definition is correct?

But another voice from the halls of Oxford, England, begs to differ with this new attempt to redefine faith as lack of evidence or knowledge.

John Lennox—a professor of mathematics at the University of Oxford, as well as an Emeritus Fellow in Mathematics and the Philosophy of Science at Oxford's Green Templeton College—has debated some of the leading voices in the movement to redefine faith as unreasonable fantasy, including both Christopher Hitchens and Richard Dawkins.

On his debate with Dawkins, Lennox noted:

> "Richard Dawkins regards faith as an evil to be eliminated; he takes all religious faith to be blind faith."

Lennox added:

"[Dawkins says that] 'scientific belief is based on publicly checkable evidence, religious faith not only lacks evidence; its independence from evidence is its joy, shouted from the rooftops' . . .

However, taking Dawkins' own advice we ask: Where is the evidence that religious faith is not based on evidence? . . .

. . . [M]ainstream Christianity will insist that faith and evidence are inseparable. Indeed, faith is a response to evidence, not a rejoicing in the absence of evidence . . . Dawkins' definition of faith as 'blind faith' turns out, therefore, to be the exact opposite of the biblical one."

> \- John Lennox, God's Undertaker

Regarding intellectual, reasoned faith versus fantasy, Lennox has noted in various statements:

"Faith is not a leap into the dark; it is the exact opposite."

"It is a commitment based on evidence."

"It is irrational to reduce all faith to blind faith and then subject it to ridicule. That provides a very anti-intellectual and convenient way of avoiding intelligent dialogue."

So which definition is true?

> Is faith really the equivalent of fantasy, or is it a commitment based on rational evidence?

1. http://www.oxforddictionaries.com/definition/english/faith

Invited to reason

In your own words, how would you describe the difference (or similarity) between faith and fantasy?

Look up 1 Peter 3:15. According to this verse, how would Peter define "reasonable faith?"

How do you think 1 Peter 3:15 will apply to Foundations of Faith?

Engage your mind = satisfying comprehension

The key concept in the idea of "reasoned faith" is that of satisfying comprehension.

One of the goals for the Foundations class is that you will have the opportunity to build satisfying comprehension of your faith in a world that will attack your faith and your beliefs.

A strong foundation for faith will engage your mind and will give you something to "rest" your faith in during the storms of life.

It is possible to have "mindless" faith without engaging our minds, but that is not the "reasoned" faith the Bible invites us to hold.

The result of mindless faith, based on emotion or feeling, is that we will end up "blown about" by every new teaching and doctrine, or our foundation will fail us in the midst of the storms of life (Eph. 4:14, Matt. 7:25-27).

But weak, unreasoned faith is not the type of faith Jesus expects from those who follow Him.

Jesus invited people to love the Lord with ALL of their minds.

"Jesus replied, 'You must love the LORD your God with all your heart, all your soul, and all your mind.'"
Matthew 22:37, NLT

"And you must love the LORD your God with all your heart, all your soul, all your mind, and all your strength."
Mark 12:30, NLT

Consider the application of these verses to our lives as students:

Why would we love the Lord with all of our minds in an AP math or science class, yet be satisfied with only a Sunday school lesson in Bible class?

As you take this course, you will be invited to engage in difficult thinking and to "dig deep."

Your faith will be challenged in this course, but the goal is that it will come out stronger as a result.

So what is "satisfying comprehension," and what will it take for us to engage our minds and reach "satisfying comprehension," both individually and as a community?

13

Why do foundations matter?
What does it say?
Matthew 7:24-27, Luke 6:47-49

Foundations determine the footprint of a building, the height of a building, the strength of a building, and the endurance of a building. Special foundations are developed and implemented for areas where storms or earthquakes are prevalent.

Foundations are often somewhat invisible, and they can easily be taken for granted. However, a well-designed foundation can make the difference between catastrophic problems in the future or a home that stands firm in the midst of a storm.

If a foundation lacks integrity either through poor design, subpar materials, or shoddy craftsmanship, then the building and those who utilize it are at risk.

So while foundations are often seen as tedious or lacking in artistic glamour, they are vital to the lasting integrity of the building.

We live in a generation in which the very definition of faith is being shaken, and we must make the most of this opportunity to build the foundation of our life with integrity, objectivity, and reason.

Reflection

1. What is the application for our faith?

2. What are the storms you believe your faith faces in this generation?

3. For the sake of this course, the word "foundations" is defined as "beliefs that we find trustworthy." What are some of the current foundations you are building your life upon? List them in the space below.

What does the Bible say about foundations?

Reflection

4. According to Luke 6:48, what is one characteristic of a strong foundation? What is the implication of this characteristic as it applies to what will be expected of you in this class?

5. According to Matthew 7:25, what is one promise the Bible gives regarding strong foundations?

6. What promise does Jesus make in Luke 6:49 regarding the life that fails to build a foundation upon His teaching?

7. In your own words, describe what you think it would look like to determine whether the words of Jesus are trustworthy enough to build the foundation of your life upon. What steps would you need to take to make this determination?

8. What is the application for you as you approach this class?

9. What is the application for you as you prepare for the rest of your life?

10. What do we need to do to build a strong foundation for learning together?

"You intended to harm me, but God
intended it for good to accomplish what is
now being done, the saving of many lives."
                              Genesis 50:20, NIV

What is faith?

Does faith impact whether or not something is true?

The first learning objective for this course is to ask the question, "What is faith?"

In order to understand what faith is, we must also seek to understand what faith is not.

The implication that Dawkins, Hitchens, Krauss, and others are making—by seeking to redefine faith as believing in something that has no proof—is that faith is simply built upon a number of "truth claims" rather than actual, verifiable truth.

In other words, when these men have the opportunity to play out their theories regarding faith, it results in a simple equation:

Faith = Ignorance
Science = Knowledge

From their perspective, the pursuit of knowledge is as much about stamping out the need for faith as it is about removing ignorance, as they equate faith with ignorance.

In fact, each of the "big three" atheists has stated that one of their hopes is that there would be no need for faith within the next several years.

They intend to imply that their version of redefined faith is equal to mere emotionally charged superstition or fantasy.

If that is true, then the stories from the Bible—about the creation of the world, Noah and the flood, the history of the nation of Israel, Jonah and the big fish, and even Jesus Christ's life, death, and resurrection—are diminished to superstitious fairy tales written by ignorant men.

If the Bible is merely a book written to supplement a lack of knowledge, then the entire Bible can be ignored as a superstitious fairy tale.

Notes:

"Nonsense remains nonsense, even when talked by world-famous scientists."
— John C. Lennox

Answer the following questions and be prepared to give reasons or evidence for your answers.

1. Does having faith in something change whether or not that something is real? Why or why not?

2. Can having faith in something change whether or not that something is true?
   Explain your answer with an example.

Objectivity

1. What are some things that could cloud our objectivity?

2. What would be some of the emotional baggage that our generation has with Christianity?

3. In your own words, how would you explain the difference between faith and fantasy?

"When the foundations are being destroyed, what can the righteous do?"
Psalm 11:3, NIV

My best class ever

Part I. Individual

1. What was the best class I have ever been a part of?

2. What made it the best class ever?

3. What did the teacher do to make it the best class ever?

4. What did I do to make it the best class ever?

5. What did the other students in the class do to make it the best class ever?

Part II. Pair and Share

1. Three ideas I heard from someone else that I really liked include:

2. One thing I think we should commit to as a class, in order to make this the best class ever would be:

Examíne™

SPIRITUAL FORMATION TOOL

ChristCenteredDiscipleship.com

"Everyone ought to examine themselves before they eat of the bread and drink from the cup."
1 Corinthians 11:28, NIV

 Wheaton Press
Read. Respond. Reflect.™

Where are you?

Read. Respond. Reflect.

Directions: *Read through the verses below and highlight or underline any words or phrases that seem to reflect or resonate with where you are at.*

Skeptic. Presented with the person of Christ and the gospel multiple times, I demonstrate disinterest or unbelief.

"Even after Jesus had performed so many signs in their presence, they still would not believe in him." John 12:37, NIV

Characteristics: Calloused heart, dull ears, closed eyes.

"[F]or this people's heart has grown callous, their ears are dull of hearing, they have closed their eyes." Matthew 13:15a, WEB

Christ's Next-Step Invitation: Repent. Believe.

"Then he began to denounce the cities in which most of his mighty works had been done, because they didn't repent." Matthew 11:20 ,WEB

Growth Barrier: A lack of spiritual understanding.

"When anyone hears the message about the kingdom and does not understand it, the evil one comes and snatches away what was sown in their heart. This is the seed sown along the path." Matthew 13:19, NIV

Spiritual Need: A change of mind and heart initiated by the Holy Spirit, a loving and praying friend.

"He said to them, 'This kind can come out by nothing, except by prayer and fasting.'" Mark 9:29, WEB

"As for you, you were dead in your transgressions and sins, in which you used to live when you followed the ways of this world and of the ruler of the kingdom of the air, the spirit who is now at work in those who are disobedient." Ephesians 2:1-2, NIV

Seeker. Questioning, with a desire to learn more about Jesus.

"He answered, 'And who is he, sir? Tell me, so that I may believe in him.'" John 9:36, ISV

Characteristics: A ready heart, open ears, questions with an interest to learn more about Jesus.

"Again, the next day, John was standing with two of his disciples, and he looked at Jesus as he walked, and said, 'Behold, the Lamb of God!' The two disciples heard him speak, and they followed Jesus. Jesus turned, and saw them following, and said to them, 'What are you looking for?' They said to him, 'Rabbi' (which is to say, being interpreted, Teacher), 'where are you staying?' He said to them, 'Come, and see.' They came and saw where he was staying, and they stayed with him that day. It was about the tenth hour." John 1:35-39, WEB

Christ's Next-Step Invitation: Repent. Believe.

"Now after John was taken into custody, Jesus came into Galilee, preaching the Good News of God's Kingdom, and saying, 'The time is fulfilled, and God's Kingdom is at hand! Repent, and believe in the Good News.'" Mark 1:14-15, WEB

Growth Barrier: A lack of clear presentation and understanding of the gospel, a lack of invitation.

"How, then, can people call on someone they have not believed? And how can they believe in someone they have not heard about? And how can they hear without someone preaching?" Romans 10:14, ISV

Spiritual Need: A clear gospel presentation and an invitation to believe and receive salvation.

"But to all who did receive him, who believed in his name, he gave the right to become children of God." John 1:12, ESV

Believer. Presented with the gospel I believe.

"He said, 'Lord, I believe!' and he worshiped him." John 9:38, WEB

Characteristics: Seed begins to germinate, shallow soil, little or no roots.

Other seeds fell on rocky ground, where they did not have much soil, and immediately they sprang up, since they had no depth of soil, but when the sun rose they were scorched. And since they had no root, they withered away. Matthew 13:5-6

Christ's Next-Step Invitation: Follow.

"And he said to them, 'Follow me, and I will make you fishers of men.'" Matthew 4:19, ESV

Growth Barrier: Lack of roots, lack of knowledge, testing, trouble, persecution.

"These in the same way are those who are sown on the rocky places, who, when they have heard the word, immediately receive   it with joy. They have no root in themselves, but are short-lived. When oppression or persecution arises because of the word,   immediately they stumble. " Mark 4:16-17, WEB

Spiritual Need: Prayer, roots, knowledge, biblical teaching, time, worship and someone to walk with them.

"Like newborn infants, long for the pure spiritual milk, that by it you may grow up into salvation." I Peter 2:2, ESV

"So then, just as you received Christ Jesus as Lord, continue to live your lives in him, rooted and built up in him, strengthened in   the faith as you were taught, and overflowing with thankfulness." Colossians 2:6-7, NIV

"We continually ask God to fill you with the knowledge of His will through all the wisdom and understanding that the Spirit gives,   so that you may live a life worthy of the Lord and please Him in every way: bearing fruit in every good work, growing in the   knowledge of God, being strengthened with all power according to His glorious might so that you may have great endurance and   patience, and giving joyful thanks to the Father, who has qualified you to share in the inheritance of His holy people in the   kingdom of light." Colossians 1:9-12, NIV.

Follower. Growing in faith and love; deepening roots and knowledge; struggling with thorns, trials, forgiveness, doubt, and perseverance.

"By this all people will know that you are my disciples, if you have love for one another." John 13:35, ESV

Characteristics: Beginning to push through the soil, struggling with thorns and weeds.

"Others fell among thorns. The thorns grew up and choked them." Matthew 13:7, WEB

"And calling the crowd to him with his disciples, he said to them, 'If anyone would come after me, let him deny himself and take up his cross and follow me.'" Mark 8:34, ESV

Christ's Next-Step Invitation: Deny self; pick up cross; trust, obey, and love Christ and others.

"Then Jesus said to his disciples, "If anyone desires to come after me, let him deny himself, and take up his cross, and follow me." Matthew 16:24, WEB

Growth Barrier: Thorns, worries of this life, doubt, deceitfulness of wealth, comfort, self and self-will.

"Others are those who are sown among the thorns. These are those who have heard the word, and the cares of this age, and the deceitfulness of riches, and the lusts of other things entering in choke the word, and it becomes unfruitful." Mark 4:18-19

Spiritual Need: Deny self; trials; endurance, perseverance, time, small group relationships, and accountability.

"Consider it pure joy, my brothers and sisters, whenever you face trials of many kinds, because you know that the testing of your faith produces perseverance. Let perseverance finish its work so that you may be mature and complete, not lacking anything." James 1:2-4, NIV

"Through him we have also obtained access by faith into this grace in which we stand, and we rejoice in hope of the glory of God. Not only that, but we rejoice in our sufferings, knowing that suffering produces endurance, and endurance produces character, and character produces hope." Romans 5:2-4, ESV

"These have come so that the proven genuineness of your faith—of greater worth than gold, which perishes even though refined by fire—may result in praise, glory and honor when Jesus Christ is revealed." 1 Peter 1:7, NIV

Friend. Marked by obedient love for Christ and others; may wrestle with isolation, complacency and accountability.

"You are my friends if you do what I command you." John 15:14, ESV

Characteristics: Good soil, obedience to Christ, fruit, growing faith, increasing love and perseverance in trials.

"We ought always to thank God for you, brothers and sisters, and rightly so, because your faith is growing more and more, and the love all of you have for one another is increasing. Therefore, among God's churches we boast about your perseverance and faith in all the persecutions and trials you are enduring." 2 Thessalonians 1:3-4, NIV

Christ's Next-Step Invitation: Love, obey, go, teach.

"If you love me, you will keep my commandments." John 14:15, ESV

"Jesus came to them and spoke to them, saying, 'All authority has been given to me in heaven and on earth. Go, and make disciples of all nations, baptizing them in the name of the Father and of the Son and of the Holy Spirit, teaching them to observe all things that I commanded you. Behold, I am with you always, even to the end of the age.' Amen." Matthew 28:18-20

Growth Barrier: Complacency, fear, pride, lack of vision and lack of equipping.

"Then he said to his disciples, 'The harvest indeed is plentiful, but the laborers are few.'" Matthew 9:37, WEB

"How, then, can people call on someone they have not believed? And how can they believe in someone they have not heard about? And how can they hear without someone preaching?" Romans 10:14, ISV

Spiritual Need: Vision, continued obedience, equipping, empowerment, continued spurring and accountability within community.

"…to equip his people for works of service, so that the body of Christ may be built up until we all reach unity in the faith and in the knowledge of the Son of God and become mature, attaining to the whole measure of the fullness of Christ." Eph 4:12-13

"As for you, brothers, do not grow weary in doing good." 2 Thessalonians 3:13, ESV

"Let us continue to hold firmly to the hope that we confess without wavering, for the one who made the promise is faithful. And let us continue to consider how to motivate one another to love and good deeds, not neglecting to meet together, as is the habit of some, but encouraging one another even more as you see the day of the Lord coming nearer." Hebrews 10:23-25, ISV

Fisherman. Reflecting Christ and reproducing fruit of righteousness and good works.

"Because we have heard of your faith in Christ Jesus and of the love you have for all God's people—the faith and love that spring from the hope stored up for you in heaven and about which you have already heard in the true message of the gospel that has come to you. In the same way, the gospel is bearing fruit and growing throughout the whole world—just as it has been doing among you since the day you heard it and truly understood God's grace." Colossians 1:4-6, NIV

Characteristics: Good soil, fruitfulness, harvest, influence, reflecting Christ.

"Others fell on good soil, and yielded fruit: some one hundred times as much, some sixty, and some thirty." Matthew 13:8,

Christ's Next-Step Invitation: Teach others.

"Therefore, as you go, disciple people in all nations, baptizing them in the name of the Father, and the Son, and the Holy Spirit, teaching them to obey everything that I've commanded you." Matthew 28:19-20a, ISV

Growth Barrier: Complacency, fear, pride, lack of vision, lack of equipping, weariness.

"Let's not get tired of doing what is good, for at the right time we will reap a harvest—if we do not give up." Galatians 6:9, ISV

"Think about the one who endured such hostility from sinners, so that you may not become tired and give up." Hebrews 12:3,

Spiritual Need: Perseverance, humility, faithfulness, accountability, reliable people.

"It gave me great joy when some believers came and testified about your faithfulness to the truth, telling how you continue to walk in it." 3 John 3, NIV

"And what you have heard from me in the presence of many witnesses entrust to faithful men who will be able to teach others also." 2 Timothy 2:2, ESV

Examine™ Spiritual Formation Planning Tool

More resources available at WheatonPress.com

Directions: Answer the following seven questions using the words or phrases you highlighted or underlined.

1. Where am I?
Skeptic. When presented with the gospel, I do not believe.
Seeker. Questioning, with a desire to learn more about Jesus.
Believer. Presented with the gospel, I chose to believe.
Follower. Growing in faith, love, and roots. Struggling with thorns, trials, and perseverance.
Friend. Marked by obedient love for Christ and others.
Fisherman. Reflecting Christ and bearing fruits of righteousness and good works.

2. Where would I like to be in six months?
Skeptic. When presented with the gospel, I do not believe.
Seeker. Questioning, with a desire to learn more about Jesus.
Believer. Presented with the gospel, I chose to believe.
Follower. Growing in faith, love, and roots. Struggling with thorns, trials, and perseverance.
Friend. Marked by obedient love for Christ and others.
Fisherman. Reflecting Christ and bearing fruits of righteousness and good works.

3. What invitation do I need to respond to in order to take my next step?
Skeptic. Repent.
Seeker. Repent. Believe.
Believer. Follow.
Follower. Deny self. Pick up cross. Obey. Love Christ and others.
Friend. Love. Obey. Go.
Fisherman. Teach others.

4. What barriers will I face?
Skeptic. Calloused heart, deaf ears, closed eyes.
Seeker. Lack of clear testimony. Lack of invitation.
Believer. Lack of root. Testing. Trouble. Persecution.
Follower. Thorns. Worries of this life. Deceitfulness of wealth. Comfort. Self.
Friend. Complacency. Fear. Lack of vision. Lack of equipping.
Fisherman. Complacency. Fear. Lack of vision. Lack of equipping. Weariness.

5. What spiritual needs do I have?
Skeptic. Prayer. Repentance. A believing friend.
Seeker. Receive. Believe. Salvation.
Believer. Prayer. Roots. Knowledge. Teaching. Worship. Time.
Follower. Deny self. Trials. Endurance. Perseverance. Time. Small group relationships and
    accountability.
Friend. Vision. Continued obedience. Equipping. Opportunity. Empowerment. Accountability within
    community.
Fisherman. Perseverance. Faithfulness. Reliable people.

6. What steps will I take?

7. Who will I ask to hold me accountable?

Self-Interview

Name:

1. What is the nature of reality? (What is really real?)

2. Who or what is God?

3. What is the basis for morality?

4. What is man? (What is mankind? What are human beings?)

5. Why are we here? (Where are we going?)

6. What is the purpose of human history?

7. What happens to a person at death?

8. What is the foundation or basis for your beliefs? (Why?)

9. What evidence do you have to support your decision to place your faith in that foundation?

Why start with worldview?

"Philosophy was necessary to the Greeks for righteousness, until the coming of the Lord. And now it assists towards true religion as a kind of preparatory training for those who arrived at Faith by way of demonstration. … But it may be, indeed, that philosophy was given to the Greeks immediately and primarily, until the Lord shall call the Greeks. For philosophy was a 'schoolmaster' to bring the Greek mind to Christ, as a law brought the Hebrews. Thus philosophy was a preparation, paving the way towards perfection in Christ."

Clement of Alexandria (c200), Stromateis, I. v.28

"In the beginning was the Word [logos] … "
John 1:1, NIV

"The Allegory of the Cave"
Excerpted from Book VII of The Republic, by Plato

And now, I said, let me show in a figure how far our nature is enlightened or unenlightened:—Behold! human beings living in a underground den, which has a mouth open towards the light and reaching all along the den; here they have been from their childhood, and have their legs and necks chained so that they cannot move, and can only see before them, being prevented by the chains from turning round their heads.

Above and behind them a fire is blazing at a distance, and between the fire and the prisoners there is a raised way; and you will see, if you look, a low wall built along the way, like the screen which marionette players have in front of them, over which they show the puppets.

I see.

And do you see, I said, men passing along the wall carrying all sorts of vessels, and statues and figures of animals made of wood and stone and various materials, which appear over the wall? Some of them are talking, others silent.

You have shown me a strange image, and they are strange prisoners.

Like ourselves, I replied; and they see only their own shadows, or the shadows of one another, which the fire throws on the opposite wall of the cave?

True, he said; how could they see anything but the shadows if they were never allowed to move their heads?

And of the objects which are being carried in like manner they would only see the shadows?

Why start with worldview?
"The Allegory of the Cave"

Yes, he said.

And if they were able to converse with one another, would they not suppose that they were naming what was actually before them?

Very true.

And suppose further that the prison had an echo which came from the other side, would they not be sure to fancy when one of the passers-by spoke that the voice which they heard came from the passing shadow?

No question, he replied.

To them, I said, the truth would be literally nothing but the shadows of the images.

That is certain.

And now look again, and see what will naturally follow if the prisoners are released and disabused of their error. At first, when any of them is liberated and compelled suddenly to stand up and turn his neck round and walk and look towards the light, he will suffer sharp pains; the glare will distress him, and he will be unable to see the realities of which in his former state he had seen the shadows; and then conceive some one saying to him, that what he saw before was an illusion, but that now, when he is approaching nearer to being and his eye is turned towards more real existence, he has a clearer vision,—what will be his reply?

And you may further imagine that his instructor is pointing to the objects as they pass and requiring him to name them,—will he not be perplexed?

Will he not fancy that the shadows which he formerly saw are truer than the objects which are now shown to him?

Far truer.

And if he is compelled to look straight at the light, will he not have a pain in his eyes which will make him turn away to take refuge in the objects of vision which he can see, and which he will conceive to be in reality clearer than the things which are now being shown to him?

True, he said.

And suppose once more, that he is reluctantly dragged up a steep and rugged ascent, and held fast until he is forced into the presence of the sun himself, is he not likely to be pained and irritated?

When he approaches the light his eyes will be dazzled, and he will not be able to see anything at all of what are now called realities.

Not all in a moment, he said.

He will require to grow accustomed to the sight of the upper world. And first he will see the shadows best, next the reflections of men and other objects in the water, and then the objects themselves; then he will gaze upon the light of the moon and the stars and the spangled heaven; and he will see the sky and the stars by night better than the sun or the light of the sun by day?

Certainly.

Last of all he will be able to see the sun, and not mere reflections of him in the water, but he will see him in his own proper place, and not in another; and he will contemplate him as he is.

Certainly.

He will then proceed to argue that this is he who gives the season and the years, and is the guardian of all that is in the visible world, and in a certain way the cause of all things which he and his fellows have been accustomed to behold?

Clearly, he said, he would first see the sun and then reason about him.

Why start with worldview?
"The Allegory of the Cave"

And when he remembered his old habitation, and the wisdom of the den and his fellow-prisoners, do you not suppose that he would felicitate himself on the change, and pity them?

Certainly, he would.

And if they were in the habit of conferring honors among themselves on those who were quickest to observe the passing shadows and to remark which of them went before, and which followed after, and which were together; and who were therefore best able to draw conclusions as to the future, do you think that he would care for such honors and glories, or envy the possessors of them? Would he not say with Homer,
'Better to be the poor servant of a poor master,'
and to endure anything, rather than think as they do and live after their manner?

Yes, he said, I think that he would rather suffer anything than entertain these false notions and live in this miserable manner.

Imagine once more, I said, such a one coming suddenly out of the sun to be replaced in his old situation; would he not be certain to have his eyes full of darkness?

To be sure, he said.

And if there were a contest, and he had to compete in measuring the shadows with the prisoners who had never moved out of the den, while his sight was still weak, and before his eyes had become steady

(and the time which would be needed to acquire this new habit of sight might be very considerable), would he not be ridiculous?

Men would say of him that up he went and down he came without his eyes; and that it was better not even to think of ascending; and if any one tried to loose another and lead him up to the light, let them only catch the offender, and they would put him to death.

No question, he said.

This entire allegory, I said, you may now append, dear Glaucon, to the previous argument; the prison-house is the world of sight, the light of the fire is the sun, and you will not misapprehend me if you interpret the journey upwards to be the ascent of the soul into the intellectual world according to my poor belief, which, at your desire, I have expressed—whether rightly or wrongly God knows.

But, whether true or false, my opinion is that in the world of knowledge the idea of good appears last of all, and is seen only with an effort; and, when seen, is also inferred to be the universal author of all things beautiful and right, parent of light and of the lord of light in this visible world, and the immediate source of reason and truth in the intellectual; and that this is the power upon which he who would act rationally either in public or private life must have his eye fixed.

I agree, he said, as far as I am able to understand you.

Questions and reflections:

"These are written that you may believe … "
John 20:31a, NIV

Why start with worldview?
The Gospel according to St. John
John 1:1-23, NIV

In the beginning was the Word, and the Word was with God, and the Word was God.

He was with God in the beginning.

Through him all things were made; without him nothing was made that has been made.

In him was life, and that life was the light of all mankind.

The light shines in the darkness, and the darkness has not overcome it.

There was a man sent from God whose name was John.

He came as a witness to testify concerning that light, so that through him all might believe.

He himself was not the light; he came only as a witness to the light.

The true light that gives light to everyone was coming into the world.

He was in the world, and though the world was made through him, the world did not recognize him.

He came to that which was his own, but his own did not receive him.

Yet to all who did receive him, to those who believed in his name, he gave the right to become children of God - children born not of natural descent, nor of human decision or a husband's will, but born of God.

The Word became flesh and made his dwelling among us. We have seen his glory, the glory of the one and only Son, who came from the Father, full of grace and truth.

(John testified concerning him. He cried out, saying, "This is the one I spoke about when I said, 'He who comes after me has surpassed me because he was before me.'")

Out of his fullness we have all received grace in place of grace already given.

For the law was given through Moses; grace and truth came through Jesus Christ.

No one has ever seen God, but the one and only Son, who is himself God and is in closest relationship with the Father, has made him known.

Now this was John's testimony when the Jewish leaders in Jerusalem sent priests and Levites to ask him who he was.

He did not fail to confess, but confessed freely, "I am not the Messiah."

They asked him, "Then who are you? Are you Elijah?"

He said, "I am not."

"Are you the Prophet?"

He answered, "No."

Finally they said, "Who are you? Give us an answer to take back to those who sent us. What do you say about yourself?"

John replied in the words of Isaiah the prophet, "I am the voice of one calling in the wilderness, 'Make straight the way for the Lord.'"

Interview Project

Essential Question

What are the foundations of trust, faith, and belief for people in my circles of influence?

Learning Goal

To begin exploring the foundations of faith and belief.

Part I. Interviews

Personal: Conduct a self-interview answering the nine interview questions. Write out your answers in the space provided in the workbook.

Peer and parent: Conduct interviews with one parent and with one peer who is not a part of this class. Ask each person the nine questions in the interview. Summarize each of their answers using the interview sheets provided in the workbook.

Part II. Personal reflection

Upon completion of your interviews, read and respond to the five reflection questions in the space provided in the workbook.

Reflection questions

1. Reflect on your self-interview. What did you find most interesting or surprising about your own responses to the nine interview questions?

2. What did you find most interesting or surprising about the interview responses you received from the two people you interviewed?

3. How were your interview responses similar to and/or different than the responses about what you believe impacts your attitude, actions, and behaviors on a daily basis?

4. Identify at least two areas that were similar.

5. Identify at least two areas that were different.

6. What questions did you discover that you struggled to answer?

7. What steps do you want to take this year to develop a fuller, more complete understanding of the foundations of your own personal beliefs?

Part III. Assessment of learning

Option A   Socratic dialogue: Students will present their reflections through dialogue in small groups. Students will be graded according to the "Socratic Dialogue" rubric.

Option B   Presentation: Students will present their reflection papers in class. Presentations will be approximately 2-4 minutes long. Students will be graded on content, clarity, analysis, and attentiveness to other presenters.

Option C   Paper: Write a 1-2 page reflection paper that demonstrates your interaction with the answers you received while answering the reflection questions. Students will be graded according to the proficiency rubric for content, clarity, and analysis.

Grading standard and proficiency rubric

Standard	Element not present for assessment	Does not meet standard	Meets standard at basic level	Above average in standard
	1	2	3	4
Content	Displays no apparent understanding of the reflection questions. No details provided.	Displays a limited understanding of the reflection questions. Very few details provided. No evidence of critical thinking skills.	Displays a proficient understanding of the reflection questions. Paper is somewhat simplistic, and it appears the writer has only offered basic information to cover the requirements of the assignment. Very little evidence of critical thinking skills.	Answers the reflection questions in a thorough and comprehensive way. The answers are backed up by significant details. Strong evidence of critical thinking skills.
Analysis	Provides weak or inappropriate analysis. Evidence use is irrelevant or significantly wrong.	Provides very limited analysis about the interviews. Mostly descriptive and incomplete.	Provides adequate analysis of the interviews but is overly simplistic and does not tie the responses together in a thoughtful way.	Provides effective and in-depth analysis about the interviews. Shows excellent use of critical thinking skills. Paper is well-thought-out.
Clarity	Paper is disorganized and poorly communicated. Most of the required elements are missing.	Paper is underdeveloped and simplistic, but does contain required elements of the assignment.	Paper lacks some development in its attempt to create a clear understanding of the reflection questions, but it is organized and contains the required elements of the paper.	Clear, well-developed reflection paper. Communication is well-organized and concise. The paper follows the format found in "How to write a one-page Bible paper."

Parent Interview

Name:

1. What is the nature of reality? (What is really real?)

2. Who or what is God?

3. What is the basis for morality?

4. What is man? (What is mankind? What are human beings?)

5. Why are we here? (Where are we going?)

6. What is the purpose of human history?

7. What happens to a person at death?

8. What is the foundation or basis for your beliefs? (Why?)

9. What evidence do you have to support your decision to place your faith in that foundation?

Peer Interview

Name:

1. What is the nature of reality? (What is really real?)

2. Who or what is God?

3. What is the basis for morality?

4. What is man? (What is mankind? What are human beings?)

5. Why are we here? (Where are we going?)

6. What is the purpose of human history?

7. What happens to a person at death?

8. What is the foundation or basis for your beliefs? (Why?)

9. What evidence do you have to support your decision to place your faith in that foundation?

Summary and Reflection

1. What did you find most interesting or surprising about your own responses?

2. What did you find most interesting or surprising about the interview responses you received from other people?

3. How were your interview responses similar to and/or different than the responses you received from others? Identify two areas that were similar and two areas you found different.

4. What questions do you struggle with? Explain your answer.

5. What steps do you want to take this year to develop a more complete understanding of the foundations for your own personal beliefs?

What is real?

Foundations of Faith

INVITED TO BELIEVE

Foundations of Faith I

Unit Essential Questions

1. What are the five foundations of faith?

2. How does what we believe impact how we live?

Unit Learning Objectives

A   To define and apply the basic concept of epistemology as it relates to the understanding of faith, truth, and belief

B   To identify the basic elements of a worldview and articulate the differences between materialism, idealism, monism, and theism

Unit Learning Assessments

1. Interview reflection paper and presentation

2. Written reflection assessment

3. Exam

Essential Questions

1. What is real?

2. What are the foundational perspectives on reality?

3. What are the faith foundations of an authentic materialist?

4. What are the faith foundations of a pure idealist?

5. What are the faith foundations of a complete monist?

6. What are the faith foundations of a true theist?

7. What are the faith foundations of a Christ-centered theist?

8. How does worldview impact my daily life?

9. Review: What have I learned?

10. Assessment: How will I demonstrate what I have learned?

11. Assessment review: What do I still need to learn?

What is the nature of reality?

How do we know what is real?

Metaphysics is the philosophical word to describe the study of what is real.

In this unit, we will be examining the foundation of faith through the questions "How do we we know if something is real?" and "What are the elements that make something real?" Remember, our goal is to separate true, reasoned faith from fantasy.

In the last unit, we discovered that faith simply means trust, and we learned that we must exercise at least some measure of faith in order to interact in a meaningful way with our world.

We also learned that faith is only valid if the thing we place our faith in is reliable. Therefore, if we are going to be wise builders who build our lives upon a strong and reasonable foundation, the application for us is to seek truth and investigate the reliability of our beliefs with objectivity.

If wisdom guides us to seek truth and to objectively investigate reliability, then we must ask and decide, "What is reliable? What makes one thing reliable and another thing unreliable?" To put it a different way, "What makes one thing real and another thing fantasy?"

What is real?

Another term for reliable is trustworthy.

The term used to describe something that is trustworthy or true is the term "real." What we are really asking in our metaphysical examination of reality is this question:

"What makes something trustworthy or true?"

If we want to separate faith from fantasy, then the cornerstone of our beliefs must be built upon a foundation that is true, something that is real.

If what we believe is not real, then we know it is false, untrue, or made up.

> Truth is what separates fantasy from reality.

> Faith does not change whether or not something is real.

For example, if I place my faith in something that is a lie (something that is not true), then it does not automatically become true simply because I believe in it.

Whether or not I choose to believe a fact does not change whether or not the fact remains true.

Using these terms, reality is defined as something that has ultimate and actual existence. In contrast, a false reality (or a fantasy) is something that does not have ultimate or actual existence.

When we begin asking questions about what is true or what is real, the next natural question is, "How do we know? How do we know what is actually true or what is actually real?"

> The term to describe this question— "How do you know what is real?"— is the word epistemology.

The reason we study metaphysics is to answer the question, "What makes something worthy of our trust?"

If something is trustworthy, then it is worth placing our faith in. The more trustworthy something is, the more credibility it has to help us lay a foundation for a strong, reasonable faith worth building our life upon.

Reflection

1. How would you answer the question, "What is real?"

2. How do you determine whether or not something is reliable?

3. How do you determine what makes something real versus what makes something a fantasy?

4. What is one takeaway or big idea from the reading on the previous page?

5. What are some things that were difficult to understand?

6. What are some questions you have?

Bell ringer

1. What is real?

2. How do I know if something is real?

3. Metaphysics means…

What are the two elemental components of reality?

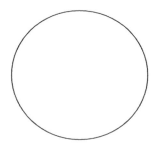

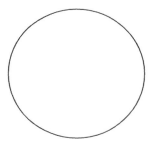

_____   _____

Plato believed:

- The spiritual realm is real.

- The physical or material realm (that which we can see, taste, and touch) is merely a shadow (Think The Matrix.)
- Plato used the word "forms" to define the ultimate reality held in the spiritual realm.

Aristotle believed:

- The spiritual realm does not exist

- The material realm is real (that which we can see, taste, touch, and measure).

- Reality, then, is measured through what we can actually experience and through physical objects (matter).
- The world has no beginning or end, but is influenced by a "Prime Mover" who is unaware of the physical world that exists and who is uninvolved with that world.

What are the foundational perspectives on reality?

What is the foundation of trust for each perspective of reality?

Materialism (Atheism)

- Materialists trust that we are complex systems of matter and electricity, subject to cause and effect and aware of our presence.
- Perfection is a completely subjective, relative concept.
- We can do whatever we prefer as long as we avoid negative natural consequences.
- Life is ultimately absurd; therefore we can create our own meaning and live out our awareness in the most personally pleasurable ways available.

Idealism (Platonism)

- Idealists trust that we are imperfect shadows trying to become one with ultimate reality, which is a state of spiritual perfection.
- We are imperfect, existing on Earth only as the various unlimited representations of imperfect images of perfection and as potential for actual existence as perfection in the real, perfect spiritual realm.
- We are personally responsible for making ourselves perfectly good, beautiful, and true in order to fully exist as perfection and actualize our escaping from eternal nonexistence.

Monism (Polytheism)

- Monists trust that we are part of all existence, and all of that which exists is already perfect as various parts of god.
- Emotions = spirit = god = truth.
- We each embody unique perspectives of god; we all have unlimited potential and power as god.
- We can embrace our preferences and seek a balance of all perspectives in order to wake up, realize, and utilize our true identity and literal unity.
- We can grow in awareness of all perspectives as the embodiment of perfection and part of our one self.
- We can learn how to see all of life as a valid and valuable part of our collective coexistence.

Theism (Monotheism)

- Theists trust that we are unique, individual creations in the image of a free, independent, personal, and all-powerful Creator.
- Although we are created in the image of the perfect God, we are independent from God and do not posses the exact nature of God.
- We are created to dwell with God and enjoy a relationship with God and God's creation.
- On Earth, we exist as imperfect beings, essentially separated from God's perfect identity and standards.
- Therefore in order to escape eternal separation from our perfect Creator and to perpetually dwell with our perfect Creator, individual perfection must be achieved and sustained.

What are the faith foundations of an authentic materialist?

Only **M**aterial is real

Materialism (Atheism)

"We are our own individual gods; there is no objective God to become, to serve, submit to, or to dwell with."

Authentic materialists trust that the composition of reality is only that which can be observed and measured materially. No actual real spirituality or spiritual realm exists. Humans are beautiful, complex systems of matter and electricity who are subjected to an intricate arrangement of pure cause and effect and who are awesomely "aware" of their immediate unfolding presence in time and space. The impression of the ideal or perfect is a completely subjective, relative concept.

Consistent materialists believe that humans can do and be whatever they prefer, so long as they avoid negative natural consequences while simultaneously and paradoxically acknowledging that this freedom is arbitrary and ultimately a facade. Life is actually an unfolding, passive adventure of random electronic reactionary impulses.

Consistent and authentic materialists unabashedly and wholeheartedly embrace the idea that life is ultimately absurd and beautifully ridiculous. Therefore genuine materialists assert that humans can attempt to "create" their own sense of adventure, purpose, and meaning. They live out their awareness in the most personally pleasurable ways available, while also hoping and seeking to avoid negative natural consequences.

What are your thoughts and questions?

Where do you see this system of belief lived out in real life?

What are the faith foundations of an authentic materialist?

The Foundational Questions	Authentic Materialist
1. What is real?	An authentic materialist ONLY trusts that the material is really real; there is no spiritual realm. The spiritual realm is a chemical/electrical figment of man's imagination, and the spiritual represents all that which we have yet to figure out how to measure and understand.
2. Who/what is God?	An authentic materialist trusts that the individual human is his/her own "god" (In other words, there is no God). There is no objective, powerful being outside of the material. God is a lie, a figment of man's creativity and imagination; He is an idea, not an existent being.
3. Who is man?	An authentic materialist trusts that human beings are unique and highly complex systems of matter and electricity that are aware of "self."
4. What is moral?	An authentic materialist trusts that morality is ultimately subjective and based on self, majority, and/or power. Morality is absurd; there is no truly objective standard for good and evil. All morality is essentially relative, based on value and agreed submission to a fabricated system of human authority and power.
5. What happens at death?	An authentic materialist trusts that one ceases to be aware of one's existence at the point of death. There is no eternal existence beyond the grave.
6. What is the meaning of history?	An authentic materialist trusts that we create our own meaning for existence. History and memory are absurd, with no objective meaning or purpose. History is simply a story of a linear sequence of events/phenomena linked by cause and effect.
7. Why are we here?	An authentic materialist trusts that we create our own meaning for life, but at the core, life is essentially absurd. There is no objective meaning or purpose. Humans should live for pleasure or the hope of pleasure. We can hope for or create positive/beneficial changes in circumstances with the least amount of negative consequences.

What are the faith foundations of a pure idealist?

Idealism (Platonism)

We are striving to exist as spiritual perfection (as "God" or as a part of "God").

Pure idealists trust that only the spiritual is the eternal fabric of prime reality.

True idealists, idea-ists, have a foundational understanding that the non-material "perfected idea" has an eternal, beautiful, true, and good weight and real-ness to it that supersedes any physical attempt to replicate and materialize this "true idea."

This understanding leads them to a greater awareness that this weight or realness of the ideal is manifested in a spiritual reality; it is merely, and often poorly, represented (re-presented) in the physical. For all of the physical world, but particularly for humans, this situation is exactly accurate. Humans are essentially "imperfect shadows" or "incomplete imitations" of the ideal spiritual reality and are literally trying to become "one with ultimate reality," which is an enlightened state of spiritual perfection.

Currently, humans are imperfect, existing on earth only as the various unlimited representations of imperfect "images" of perfection. They also exist as potential for actual eternal existence in a state of perfection in the ideal perfect spiritual realm. Humans are personally responsible for making themselves into the ideal, by becoming perfectly good, beautiful, and true, in order to exist fully and eternally as spiritual perfection and to actualize eternally escaping their nonexistence as an incomplete, shadowy replica.

What are your thoughts and questions?

Where do you see this system of belief lived out in real life?

What are the faith foundations of a pure idealist?

The Foundational Questions	Pure Idealist
1. What is real?	A pure idealist ONLY trusts that the spiritual is really real and that reality is a state of eternal spiritual perfection. The material realm is an imperfect (broken, twisted, warped) shadow of the absolutely good, beautiful, and true spiritual realm.
2. Who/what is God?	A pure idealist trusts that the impersonal, eternal, and perfect one ideal is what people call "god"; it is absolute truth, beauty, and goodness, a state of mind and being. God is the "one" that "is" perfect, absolutely and forever.
3. Who is man?	A pure idealist trusts that humans are not perfect. We are one of the infinite imperfect shadows of the real state of spiritual perfection. Humans exist simply as potential to literally become one with "god," finally existing as perfection in a state of eternal spiritual perfection.
4. What is moral?	A pure idealist trusts that all morality is objective based on the nature of the impersonal, perfect "one" ideal, which is absolute truth, beauty, and goodness.
5. What happens at death?	A pure idealist trusts that when we die, perfection is attained, and "oneness" with the ideal is achieved. We realize our potential, let go of the imperfect representation of "self," and become one with the state of spiritual perfection OR (AND) we cease to exist at all.
6. What is the meaning of history?	A pure idealist trusts that history is a record of humans striving to escape nonexistence and attain a state of spiritual perfection.
7. Why are we here?	A pure idealist trusts that we exist only to escape painful nonexistence, to achieve a state of spiritual perfection, and to exist eternally through becoming "one with the one," by being absolutely, perfectly, and spiritually good, beautiful, and true.

What are the faith foundations of a complete monist?

Monism (Polytheism)

"We are already 'god'; embrace and enjoy this truth, and stop striving to become what you already are."

Complete monists trust that both the measurable, material and mysterious, spiritual realms co-exist as one (very large) entity. Dualists, often called pantheists, assert that ALL of reality is one reality presenting itself as "dual" in nature. This duality is represented in unlimited perspectives and polarities, as experienced throughout the vast complexity and tensions of life.

For a complete monist, all of life is connected, literally. Humans are a part of all existence, and all of that which exists is already the ideal for life and thus is perfect, existing as various parts of the one entity that dualists often refer to as "god."

God, literally, is everything, and humans are a part of the everything that exists. For all of life: Emotions = Spirit = God = Truth = Life = Material = Perspective = Emotions.

The universal reality and unity of dualism is like a human body, which has many apparent distinctions and parts yet maintains a complex unity and harmony. In the literal sense, each human embodies unique perspectives of god; humans have unlimited potential and power as god or as a connected part of god. Humans can embrace their unique preferences and seek a balance of all perspectives and polarities so as to wake up, realize, and utilize their true identity and literal unity with reality. Humans (along with all creatures and all parts of reality) can grow in awareness of all perspectives as they embody the simplicity and complexity of life as a part of the one (gigantic, one) self. Humans can learn how to see all of life and all of life's tensions and polarities—the dualities of life—as a valid and valuable part of humanity's collective unity and coexistence with all that is.

What are your thoughts and questions?

Where do you see this system of belief lived out in real life?

What are the faith foundations of a complete monist?

The Foundational Questions	Complete Monist
1. What is real?	A complete monist trusts that the spiritual and the material are BOTH real, existing as one entity. The spiritual realm and material realm both exist, but are one and the same; there is no true separation or distinction between the two realms. Reality is dual in nature, like a coin. All of existence is one interconnected unity that unfolds in various forms.
2. Who/what is God?	A complete monist trusts that everything is "god," that everything and everybody is an integral, interconnected part of the unity of life called "god." Existence and reality is what people would call "god." Life and the cosmos is filled with dualities; thus "god" has a "dual" nature in essence and being.
3. Who is man?	A complete monist trusts that a human is a unique, unrepeatable part of "god." We are a part of the body of the universe and entirety of reality referred to as "god."
4. What is moral?	A complete monist trusts that morality is completely subjective, based solely on one's individual preference as a part of the interconnected universal reality called "god." Like "god," morality is dual in nature, e.g., positive and negative energy, creative and destructive forces, dark and light, etc.
5. What happens at death?	A complete monist trusts that when a human "dies," he or she literally "morphs" into another part of existence and another component of reality, which is "god."
6. What is the meaning of history?	A complete monist trusts that we are connected to history as part of the one existence, which is "god."
7. Why are we here?	A complete monist trusts that every human has the opportunity to continue the experience of being various components of reality—of "god"—forever. We are here to reach our full potential as a part of the divine existence and unity of "god."

What are the faith foundations of a true theist?

Theism (Monotheism)

M + S are both real

"We are unique, individual creations hoping to become perfect so as to dwell with God, our perfect creator."

True theists trust that both the spiritual and the material are components of prime reality, and while they are both interdependent and dependent on one another, they are also mysteriously intradependent: dependent within each other.

Humans are unique, individual creations in the image of a free, independent, personal, and all-powerful creator, often referred to as God. Although humans are created in the image of the one perfect God as individual, distinct creations of God, humans are actually independent beings from God and do not possess the exact nature of God.

Humans are created to dwell freely with God and enjoy a relationship with God and God's creation. On Earth, humans exist as imperfect (incomplete) beings, essentially separated from God's perfect identity and standards. Therefore, in order for humans to escape eternal separation from their perfect creator and to dwell perpetually with their perfect creator, individual perfection (fullness) must be achieved and sustained.

What are your thoughts and questions?

Where do you see this system of belief lived out in real life?

What are some foundational distinctions of a true theist?

The Foundational Questions	True Theist
1. What is real?	A true theist trusts that the spiritual and the material are both real, yet dependent and interdependent on each other. The spiritual realm and material realm are both independently real, yet coexist and interact in various degrees and in various ways.
2. Who/what is God?	A true theist trusts that there is a God that is the all-powerful creator, sustainer, and giver of all of life. God is perfect and good. God is personal and has personality. God has full authority. God is the standard for and author of morality.
3. Who is man?	A true theist trusts that humans are a distinct creation made in the image of God but not possessing the exact nature of God.
4. What is moral?	A true theist trusts that morality is objective, based on the personal, all-powerful nature of God, who is perfect and good. God (and God's Word) is the standard for and author of morality.
5. What happens at death?	A true theist trusts that when we die, we obtain individual perfection and exist eternally in continual relationship with the perfect, personal God, or we remain in a broken, imperfect state and exist separated from God.
6. What is the meaning of history?	A true theist trusts that history is a "linear, meaningful sequence of events leading to the fulfillment of God's purposes for man" in an open system (James Sire, *The Universe Next Door*). History is THE story of God's interaction with mankind. Humans are independent, autonomous, and gregarious, possessing will and identity as self.
7. Why are we here?	A true theist trusts that the reason humans exist is to enjoy and experience a meaningful, personal relationship with the creator and sustainer of life. We exist so that we can bring joy and honor to God through worshiping God, through relationship with God, and through serving God and others.

What are the faith foundations of a true, Christ-centered theist?

Christ-centered theism (True Christianity)

M + S are both real

Jesus is the author and finisher of the faith.
Jesus became our perfection for us and offers us forgiveness and true freedom to become His reflections.

"They have torn the soul of Christ into silly strips."
G. K. Chesterton

Christ-centered theists trust that humans were created as integrated (whole) beings, material in nature, while in relationship with our supernatural creator. Humans are unique, individual creations in the image of a free, independent, personal, and all-powerful creator.

Although humans are created in the image of the one perfect God, humans—as individual, distinct creations of God—are actually independent from God and do not possess the exact nature of God. Instead, we were created to reflect the image of our supernatural creator.

Humans are created to dwell freely with God and enjoy a relationship with God and God's creation.

On Earth, humans exist as imperfect (incomplete) beings, essentially separated from God's perfect identity and standards.

Therefore, in order for humans to escape eternal separation from their perfect creator and to dwell perpetually with their perfect creator, individual perfection (fullness) was achieved through the life, death, and resurrection of Christ.

Jesus Christ is the author and the finisher of all truth. Jesus became our perfection and offers forgiveness and true freedom through faith and trust in Him. Forgiveness offers us full freedom to return to our divine purpose of reflecting Christ.

What are your thoughts and questions?

Where do you see this system of belief lived out in real life?

What are some foundational distinctions of a Christ-centered theist?

The Foundational Questions	Christ-Centered Theist
1. What is real?	A true, Christ-centered theist trusts that the spiritual and the material are both real, yet independent of and interdependent with each other. The spiritual realm and material realm are both independently real, yet coexist and interact independently and interdependently in various degrees and in various ways. Jesus is the ultimate reflection of reality. Jesus is 100 percent fully God and 100 percent fully man.
2. Who/what is God?	A Christ-centered theist trusts that there is a triune God that is the all-powerful creator, sustainer, and giver of all of life. God is perfect and good. God is personal and has personality. God has full authority. God is the standard for and author of morality. Jesus is God. All things were created and brought to life by Jesus. Jesus is perfect and lived a perfect life. Jesus is the standard and author of morality.
3. Who is man?	A Christ-centered theist trusts that humans are a distinct creation, made in the image of God but not possessing the exact nature of God. Man is created by Jesus for the purpose of reflecting the image of God.
4. What is moral?	A Christ-centered theist trusts that morality is objective, based on the personal, all-powerful nature of God, who is perfect and good. God (and God's Word) is the standard for and author of morality. Jesus is the creator of and personification of truth. The Bible is the written revelation of God's truth.
5. What happens at death?	A Christ-centered theist trusts that when we die, we obtain individual perfection and exist eternally in continual relationship with the perfect personal God, or we remain in a broken, imperfect state and exist, separated from God. In essence, when we die, we actualize "self" and exist with God. Because of the sacrifice of Jesus, we have the opportunity to be in a right relationship with God, both now and after we die.
6. What is the meaning of history?	A Christ-centered theist trusts that history is a "linear, meaningful sequence of events leading to the fulfillment of God's purposes for man" in an open system (James Sire, *The Universe Next Door*). History is THE story of God's interaction with mankind. Humans are independent, autonomous, and gregarious, possessing will and identity as self. The Bible is God's record and revelation of human history, pointing us to Jesus (Acts 17:26-27).
7. Why are we here?	A Christ-centered theist trusts that the reason humans exist is to enjoy and experience a meaningful, personal relationship with the creator and sustainer of life. We exist in order to enjoy, pursue, steward, and reflect God's kingdom. We exist so we can bring joy and honor to God through worshiping Him, through relationship with God, and through serving God and others. We are designed, called, and commissioned to reflect Jesus.

How does worldview impact my daily life?

Why does any of this matter?

At first glance, it is easy to wonder how our answers to the seven questions apply to our daily lives, yet consider that…

How we view the world impacts our life every moment of every day.

Our foundational beliefs regarding morality and perfection directly influence our daily behavior and decisions, as well as how we view ourselves and make sense of the actions of others.

How does understanding the foundations of worldview equip me to make sense of the world?

- Understanding the nature of reality provides us with a filter or a lens that brings clarity.

- Understanding how people view reality equips us to understand others, by providing meaning to the words they use.

- Understanding what or who people trust, equips us to interpret the messages we receive from the culture in which we live.

- Understanding what we trust equips us to understand ourselves and our own motivations.

- Understanding equips us with confidence.

Lack of understanding can lead to confusion, frustration, fear, nervousness, and other paralyzing emotions.

Lack of understanding can also lead to poor decision-making.

For example, imagine ordering food from a restaurant without being able to read the language in which the menu is written. Without understanding the words, you would simply be guessing.

Seeing the world through the lens of reality solidifies our faith, equips us to make sense of the world around us, and also equips us to make wise decisions by operating with understanding and confidence.

In his letter to the early church in Colossae, the apostle Paul warned us not to be taken captive by "hollow and deceptive" philosophies that are not centered on Christ.

See to it that no one takes you captive through hollow and deceptive philosophy, which depends on human tradition and the elemental spiritual forces of this world rather than on Christ.
- Colossians 2:8, NIV

The impact of worldview

The Bible teaches that we were created as integrated beings who lived in the fullness of reality. We were created by our supernatural creator to reflect Him with our natural lives in wholeness and authenticity. However, rebellion caused a disintegration (separation) in our relationship with God and in how we view the world. As a result, we view the world through a disintegrated lens. For some, the disintegration causes us to view the world only through the lens of the material aspects of reality. For others, disintegration causes us to view the world only through the lens of the supernatural aspects of reality.

It could be said that each worldview has a "strip of the truth": truth that is found in the full reality of Jesus Christ, who is both 100 percent divine and 100 percent human. G. K. Chesterton once wrote, "They have torn the soul of Christ into silly strips." From the perspective of a Christ-centered theist, this quote explains the view of reality of other worldviews.

How does worldview impact my daily life?

What does the Bible say about how reality has become disintegrated?

Romans 3:23 says: I Corinthians 4:4 says:

What is the implication?   How does this apply?

How we view the world determines how we think, act, and feel.

Consider the following applications and scenarios from the perspective of each worldview.

Assessment review

Part I. Demonstrate knowledge

- Label the circles as representing each of the perspectives on the nature of reality.

- Answer the questions for each of the four faith foundations.

Part II. Demonstrate understanding

Be able to identify, define, and interact with the following words and concepts:

- The difference between faith and fantasy (reasonable and unreasonable faith)

- Metaphysics

- The basic beliefs of Plato

- The basic beliefs of Aristotle

- The two primary elemental components of reality

- The four foundational perspectives of reality

- Epistemology

- Pluralism

- Relativism

- Foundational beliefs and influences on morality

Part III. Demonstrate application

Be prepared to demonstrate an understanding of how foundational systems of belief impact daily life.

Materialism

1. What is the nature of reality? What is really real?
2. Who is God? What is God?
3. What is the basis of morality? (Who decides what is right/wrong?)
4. Who/what is man? What is mankind?
5. What happens to man at death?
6. What is the meaning/purpose of human history?
7. Why are we here? Where are we going?

Idealism

1. What is the nature of reality? What is really real?
2. Who is God? What is God?
3. What is the basis of morality? (Who decides what is right/wrong?)
4. Who/what is man? What is mankind?
5. What happens to man at death?
6. What is the meaning/purpose of human history?
7. Why are we here? Where are we going?

Monism

1. What is the nature of reality? What is really real?
2. Who is God? What is God?
3. What is the basis of morality? (Who decides what is right/wrong?)
4. Who/what is man? What is mankind?
5. What happens to man at death?
6. What is the meaning/purpose of human history?
7. Why are we here? Where are we going?

Theism

1. What is the nature of reality? What is really real?
2. Who is God? What is God?
3. What is the basis of morality? (Who decides what is right/wrong?)
4. Who/what is man? What is mankind?
5. What happens to man at death?
6. What is the meaning/purpose of human history?
7. Why are we here? Where are we going?

The Foundational Questions	My Trust List	Some major cultural, religious, social, and personal connections
1. What is real?	I trust (believe) that	
2. Who/what is God?	I trust (believe) that	
3. Who is man?	I trust (believe) that	
4. What is moral?	I trust (believe) that	
5. What happens at death?	I trust (believe) that	
6. What is the meaning of history?	I trust (believe) that	
7. Why are we here?	I trust (believe) that	

Notes and dialogue

55

Notes and dialogue

What is true?

Foundations of Faith

Unit Essential Questions

1. What is true?

2. Does an objective standard for truth exist?

Unit Learning Objectives

A. To understand the differences between various approaches to truth, including objective and subjective, inclusive and exclusive, and exegetical and eisegetical

B. To understand that truth is not subjective, but defined objectively through the person of Christ

Unit Learning Assessments

1. Socratic dialogue

2. Written reflection paper

3. Exam

Essential Questions

1. What is true, and what makes something true?

2. Can truth be objectively established, and does a standard for truth exist?

3. What is perfect, and who defines perfection?

4. What is morality, and who defines morality?

5. What is the law of noncontradiction, and how does it apply to the concept of truth?

6. Can the existence of an absolute standard be proven?

7. What are the arguments for the existence of God?

8. What do Christ-centered theists believe about the origin of truth?

9. What are two different approaches to understanding God's written revelation?

10. Review: What have I learned?

11. Assessment: How will I demonstrate what I have learned?

12. Assessment review: What do I still need to learn?

What is true?
How do you know whether something is true?

If we must exercise at least some measure of faith in order to interact in a meaningful way with our world, and if faith is only valid if the thing we put it in is reliable, and if wisdom guides us to seek truth and investigate reliability with objectivity, then we must ask and decide:

- What is true?
- What makes something true?
- What makes something trustworthy?
- Is there an objective or subjective standard for truth?

Bell ringer

1. How would you define truth?

2. How do you know whether something is true?

3. What are some of the elements that make something true?

What is true?

How do you know whether something is true?

In this unit, we will examine what the fundamental elements that make something true are, whether there is an objective standard that defines truth, and how the standard has been revealed to us, so that we can know truth.

Define the term:

What is *true?*

What is *truth?*

"What is truth?" retorted Pilate.
- John 18:38, NIV

Why does it matter?

"Then you will know the truth, and the truth will set you free."
- John 8:32, NIV

What makes something true?

How do you know?

Is something true because I believe it? Or do I believe something because it is true?

What is the difference?

61

What makes something trustworthy?

1. List the characteristics or factors that would lead you to decide whether or not something is worthy of your trust.

2. What are the fundamental elements that determine whether or not something is "true?"

3. How do you know?

4. What is the difference between subjective and objective truth?

5. Explain in your own words why this matters.

Foundational terms and concepts to build common understanding

Metaphysics

Epistemology

Belief

Pluralism

For example:

Relativism

Key concept: Exclusive is when…   Key concept: Inclusive is when …

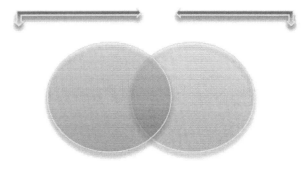

Can truth be objectively established?
How is truth revealed?

What is your name?

List at least five reasons for how you know.

Premise: In order for truth to be known, it must be _____

Application: In order for God to be known, He must choose to _____

Notes, examples, and dialogue

Does an absolute standard for truth exist?
Can truth be objectively established?

What (or who) ultimately determines what is true?

What is perfect and who defines perfection?
What is the application of truth?

- How does a materialist define perfection?

- How does an idealist define perfection?

- How does a monist define perfection?

- How does a theist define perfection?

- How does a Christ-centered theist define perfection?

How is perfection attained?

Axiom 1. IF a perfect God has perfect standards, THEN, by necessity, one must be perfect in order to dwell with this perfect God.

Axiom 2. IF a being is imperfect, THEN, by necessity, that same being cannot become perfectly perfect if left to himself or herself, because by necessity, one would need to be perfect in order to do this perfectly.

How is perfection attained?

Putting the axioms into practice:

How would each of the worldviews use a dirty rag to clean a window?

- A materialist

- An idealist

- A monist

- A theist

- A Christ-centered theist

What makes Christ-centered theism distinct?

What is moral, and who defines morality?
What is the application of truth?

- How does a materialist define morality?

- How does an idealist define morality?

- How does a monist define morality?

What is morality, and who defines morality?

- How does a theist define morality?

- How does a Christ-centered theist define morality?

Application

- If morality is subjective, then:

- If morality is objective, then:

How is morality determined?

Axiom I. IF there is no spiritual realm or objective reality, THEN morality, by necessity, has to be internally relative in a closed system.

Axiom 2. IF morality is internally relative in a closed system, THEN, by necessity, the concepts of right and wrong, good and evil, fair and unfair, are arbitrary and absurd. Everything is ultimately based on personal preference.

- What do truth and morality automatically become if we use this approach?

- Why?

- What are the consequences and/or implications of this system of belief?

What is the law of noncontradiction?

Using basic logic, is truth inclusive or exclusive?

Two reasons that we resist the concept include:

Ironically, even in the worldview that would claim a level of inclusiveness (monism), its system of belief would exclude the possibility of _____. Explain the reason for your answer.

Why does this matter?

1.

2.

3.

How does the law of noncontradiction apply to each of the worldviews?

A materialist would say:

The law of noncontradiction would say:

An idealist would say:

The law of noncontradiction would say:

A monist would say:

The law of noncontradiction would say:

A theist would say:

The law of noncontradiction would say:

A Christ-centered theist would say:

The law of noncontradiction would say:

Application and conclusion:

Can the existence of an absolute standard be proven? (Why or why not?)

1.   **What is the teleological argument?**

    • What are some examples of this argument?

2.   **What is the cosmological argument?**

    • What are some examples of this argument?

    • What is the second law of thermodynamics?

    • How does this apply?

Additional arguments

3.   What is the moral argument?

4.   What is the ontological argument?

Reflection: Which arguments seem reasonable?

Why?

Examining the arguments

Research and become an "expert" on an argument you want to examine, in order to see whether it is reasonable, and then be able to explain it to someone else. You may use this website as a source: tinyurl.com/20arguments

- The argument from desire

    Summarize:

    Evaluate:

- Cosmological argument (Kalam argument)

    Summarize:

    Evaluate:

- Moral argument

    Summarize:

    Evaluate:

- Pascal's wager

    Summarize:

    Evaluate:

What are the arguments for the existence of God?
Collaborative assignment

Directions

Use the website tinyurl.com/20arguments to analyze one of the arguments for the existence of God that will be assigned to your group.

Your task is to examine and then summarize the argument using the website as a resource, and then evaluate the argument by discussing its strengths and weaknesses.

Once you are knowledgeable on the argument, you will be reassigned to a new group and will need to be prepared to present your findings to the rest of the class in a meaningful and memorable way.

Continue the conversation at home

Directions: We have been examining some arguments for the existence of God in class this week. Your next step is to engage your parents using the following two questions. Write down their responses below.

1. Present one or both of your parents with this scenario: You are at a coffee shop with a friend, and your friend asks, "Why do you believe in God?" How would you answer this question? Summarize your parent's (or parents') response. Use bullet points or an outline form.

2. Share one of the arguments for the existence of God that we discussed (teleological, cosmological, moral, desire) with your parents. Ask them to evaluate the argument. Where do they think it is strong? Do they see any weaknesses in the argument?

.

What do Christ-centered theists believe about the origin of truth?

1. What does John 1:3 say about the origination of truth?

2. What does John 14:6a say about the personification of truth?

3. Explain this statement: "Truth is not objective or subjective; it is personified."

4. What does John 18:37 say about the revelation of truth?

What do Christ-centered theists believe about the revelation of truth?

Can God's revelation be trusted?

How do you know?

Can God's revelation be perfect?

How do you know?

The Bible claims that God is perfectly revealed through Scripture.

- What does 2 Timothy 3:16-17 say?

- What does Hebrews 4:12 say?

The Bible claims that God is perfectly revealed through Jesus.

- What does Matthew 1:20 say?

- What does John 14:9b say?

- What does John 10:30 say?

- What does 1 Peter 2:22 say?

If an absolute standard of truth has been revealed, what should our approach be toward discovering and applying it? Explain your answer.

What are two different approaches to understanding God's written revelation?

- What is an eisegetical response to the revelation of God's truth?

- What is an exegetical response to the revelation of God's truth?

How does understanding all that we have learned equip us for practical life?

1. It equips us to:

2. It equips us to:

3. It equips us to:

4. It equips us to:

5. It equips us with:

Understanding the foundations of faith will not only solidify our own faith, but it will equip us to make sense of the world around us and the revelation of God to us.

> *See to it that no one takes you captive through hollow and deceptive philosophy, which depends on human tradition and the elemental spiritual forces of this world rather than on Christ.*
> *- Colossians 2:8, NIV*

Our foundational beliefs regarding morality and perfection directly influence our daily behavior and decisions. Our foundational beliefs regarding the trustworthiness of the Bible as God's perfect revelation should influence how we approach and apply it to our lives.

Application:

Since our behavior is influenced by our beliefs, in order to change an action, we must first identify our beliefs and renew (or change) our mind. To experience true change in my life, I must begin by changing my mind about how I view the world.

> *Do not conform to the pattern of this world, but be transformed by the renewing of your mind. Then you will be able to test and approve what God's will is—his good, pleasing and perfect will.*
> *- Romans 12:2, NIV*

Reflection:

Video notes and dialogue

Video notes and dialogue

Compare and contrast the Christ-centered theistic beliefs about truth with the views of moral relativism and pluralism. Give examples.

- What is similar?

- What is different?

- What makes Christ-centered theism distinct?

- What view do you find more rational? Explain your answer.

- What questions do you still have?

Learning assessment options

- Option A. Exam.

- Option B. Formative and summative paper.

- Option C. Formative paper, summative paper, and exam.

Formative paper

Following the guidelines for a one-page paper and using specific references, answer the following questions:

Question 1: "In what ways have I been influenced by moral relativism in my generation?"

Question 2: "How, if at all, has this unit impacted my perspective of Jesus and my view of absolute truth?"

Summative paper

1. Choose two worldviews and explain the concepts of pluralism, relativism, exclusivity, and inclusivity as they relate to the foundations of faith through the lenses of these worldviews. How does each worldview approach the law of noncontradiction? What evidence leads you to believe that each worldview is either rational or irrational?

1. From the perspective of a true, Christ-centered theist, how does God reveal truth through the Word of God?

2. What did you learn about Jesus through the Scriptures studied in this unit?

3. How would your reading of God's Word change if you approached Jesus as the embodiment of truth and the Bible as God's true revelation? How would Jesus become the center of everything in Scripture? Explain your answer through the lens of an eisegetical versus an exegetical approach.

Exam

Assessment of learning

There are three primary types of assessments that you may participate in during this unit:

Formative assessments: These are personal reflections, designed to invite you to personalize your learning. They are nongraded and demonstrate your learning process and progression.

Summative assessments: These are graded demonstrations of your understanding and ability to articulate the concepts you have been taught. These grades are not based on your personal beliefs, but on the demonstration of your interaction with and understanding of the material taught in this unit through the lens of the following skills.

Specific measured standards for this paper include:

- [CCSS.ELA-Literacy.W.9-10.1] Write arguments to support claims in an analysis of substantive topics or texts, using valid reasoning and relevant and sufficient evidence.

- [CCSS.ELA-Literacy.W.9-10.1a] Introduce precise claim(s), distinguish the claim(s) from alternate or opposing claims, and create an organization that establishes clear relationships among claim(s), counterclaims, reasons, and evidence.

- [CCSS.ELA-Literacy.W.9-10.1b] Develop claim(s) and counterclaims fairly, supplying evidence for each while pointing out the strengths and limitations of both in a manner that anticipates the audience's knowledge level and concerns.

- [CCSS.ELA-Literacy.W.9-10.1c] Use words, phrases, and clauses to link the major sections of the text, create cohesion, and clarify the relationships between claim(s) and reasons, between reasons and evidence, and between claim(s) and counterclaims.

- [CCSS.ELA-Literacy.W.9-10.1d] Establish and maintain a formal style and objective tone while attending to the norms and conventions of the discipline in which [you] are writing.

- [CCSS.ELA-Literacy.W.9-10.1e] Provide a concluding statement or section that follows from and supports the argument presented.

Student learning exam: This demonstration of learning is designed to measure your knowledge and understanding through multiple choice questions.

Foundations of Faith Unit Two Assessment

Proficiency scale

Learning objectives of the paper will be measured on the following scale of proficiency.

Standard	Element not present for assessment — 1	Does not meet standard — 2	Meets standard at basic level — 3	Proficient in standard — 4
CCSS.ELA-Literacy.W.9-10.1a Introduce precise claim(s), distinguish the claim(s) from alternate or opposing claims, and create an organization that establishes clear relationships among claim(s), counterclaims, reasons, and evidence. *Introduction: Minimum 4 sentences.*	Element Not Present	Demonstrates little, if any knowledge or understanding of worldview material or definitions explicitly taught in class.	Demonstrates basic knowledge or understanding of material explicitly taught in class.	Demonstrates knowledge or understanding of worldview material and definitions explicitly taught in class.
CCSS.ELA-Literacy.W.9-10.1b Develop claim(s) and counterclaims fairly, supplying evidence for each while pointing out the strengths and limitations of both in a manner that anticipates the audience's knowledge level and concerns. *Q1. Choose two worldviews and explain the concepts of pluralism, relativism, exclusivity, and inclusivity as they relate to the foundations of faith through the lens of those worldviews.*	Element Not Present	Demonstrates little, if any knowledge or understanding of worldview material or definitions explicitly taught in class.	Demonstrates basic knowledge or understanding of material explicitly taught in class.	Demonstrates knowledge or understanding of worldview material and definitions explicitly taught in class.
CCSS.ELA-Literacy.W.9-10.1c Use words, phrases, and clauses to link the major sections of the text, create cohesion, and clarify the relationships between claim(s) and reasons, between reasons and evidence, and between claim(s) and counterclaims. *Q1. How does each worldview approach the law of non-contradiction? What evidence leads you to believe that worldview is either rational or irrational?*	Element Not Present	Demonstrates little, if any knowledge or understanding of how two worldviews relate to the law of non-contradiction.	Demonstrates basic knowledge or understanding of how two worldviews relate to the law of non-contradiction with little to no evidence regarding part II.	Demonstrates knowledge or understanding of how two worldviews relate to the law of non-contradiction and provides evidence for conclusion.
CCSS.ELA-Literacy.W.9-10.1d Establish and maintain a formal style and objective tone while attending to the norms and conventions of the discipline in which they are writing. *Q2. From the perspective of a true Christ-centered Theist: How does God reveal truth through the Word of God?*	Element Not Present	Demonstrates basic knowledge or understanding of how a Christ-centered Theist views the how God reveals truth.	Demonstrates knowledge or understanding of how a Christ-centered Theist views the how God reveals truth.	Demonstrates Level 3 knowledge and understanding and demonstrates higher-level critical thinking regarding how a Christ-centered Theist views the how God reveals truth.
CCSS.ELA-Literacy.W.9-10.1e Provide a concluding statement or section that follows from and supports the argument presented. Q3.Q4. Personal Reflection.	Element Not Present	Demonstrates basic knowledge or understanding of material explicitly taught in class and provides personal reflection.	Demonstrates basic knowledge or understanding of material explicitly taught in class and provides personal reflection while demonstrating understanding of both an eisegetical and exegetical approaches to scripture.	Demonstrates Level 3 knowledge and understanding and includes material pulled from additional paragraphs to provide a comprehensive conclusion.

Proficiency scale
Personal application

Learning objectives in the "Application" section of the paper will be based on the following scale of proficiency.

0	1	2
Not attempted.	Student demonstrates a generic or simplistic application. Sentences or thoughts are not complete or do not meet the minimum of four sentences for a complete paragraph. Student demonstrates basic (if any) interaction with the material in a personal way. Thoughts are generic or incomplete in nature.	Evidence is given that the student interacted with the significance of his or her beliefs in a meaningful way. References are made to the student's beliefs and how those beliefs impact his or her life. Interaction demonstrates higher level thought, critical thinking, and personal reflection. Thoughts are complete and demonstrate an interaction with the material in paragraphs that are a minimum of four sentences.

Notes and dialogue

87

Notes and dialogue

What are the foundations of Christ-centered faith?

Foundations of Faith

Unit Essential Questions

1. How do Christ-centered theists answer the seven critical questions?

2. What is an integrated life?

Unit Learning Objectives

A. To explore what the Bible teaches about God's design and purpose for life

B. To understand the distinction between justification and sanctification from a Christ-centered theistic perspective

C. To actively engage in a positive and meaningful peer-led dialogue about faith and belief

Unit Learning Assessments

1. Socratic dialogue

2. Written reflection paper

Essential Questions

1. What is the difference between a discussion and a dialogue?

2. What is man, and why are we here?

3. What is moral, why do people die, and what happens at death?

4. What is the standard for perfection?

5. Why did Jesus die?

6. What is the fullness of Christ, and how does it apply to my everyday life?

7. Review: What have I learned?

8. Assessment: How will I communicate what I have learned?

What is the difference between a discussion and a dialogue?
How will we create a safe environment for dialogue about faith and belief?

Socratic dialogue

The goal of the Socratic dialogue method is to give the responsibility of teaching, differentiation, and learning to the students. The more you own the experience, the more meaningful and memorable it will be. These are the types of conversations that you will have outside of the classroom for the rest of your life.

Here are four keys to experiencing an engaging and meaningful Socratic dialogue:

- First, make sure that you have read the day's material on your own, outside of class.

- Second, when you read, make sure that you note points with which you agree, have questions, or disagree. Sometimes it is helpful to use differently colored pens or highlighters to help you remember where to find your notes and to organize your thoughts during the dialogue.

- Third, the role of the dialogue leader is to ensure that everyone is engaged in the dialogue.

  Note: It is the role of the dialogue leader to ask great questions, not to have all the answers. The dialogue leader should be asking questions and ensuring that others are participating. Over the course of the entire semester, every student should have the responsibility to lead.

- Fourth, one student will have the task of recording the group's conversation by marking on a diagram when a student talks and to whom that student is talking.

Ground Rules:

Chapter 1. Created to Reflect
Dialogue guide

Excerpts from the reading

"We are made in the Creator's own image! The purpose of our lives, therefore, is to reflect the character of the Creator and to honor Him through our lives and our relationship with the rest of creation."

"But many of us go through our lives and never consider the amazing ramifications of our design. We care only for our own happiness and self-interest. Our lives reflect these selfish and small-minded priorities instead of the original purpose for which we were designed."

"In his book, *Confessions*, the fourth century theologian St. Augustine wrote:

> "Men go abroad to wonder at the heights of mountains, at the huge waves of the sea, at the long courses of the rivers, at the vast compass of the ocean, at the circular motions of the stars and they pass by themselves without wondering."

"Our value is not self-earned; rather, it is inherently placed in us by the One who knit us together by hand and marked us with His fingerprints."

"God made you. He created you as a reflection of His image. You belong to Him in both body and spirit."

"You and I are valuable. Not because of anything we have accomplished or because of a particular skill or talent that we might possess, but because of Who created us and the purpose we were created to accomplish. We are masterpieces created by the greatest Artist of all time and put on display for the purpose of reflecting His image, majesty, wisdom, and character for all to see."

"The apostle Paul, under the inspiration of the Spirit of God, wrote:

> 'We are God's *poiema*, created in Christ Jesus to do good works, which He prepared in advance for us to do. Ephesians 2:10 (NIV, adapted).'"

Reflection questions

1. What ideas or images stood out to you in this chapter?

2. Have you ever considered what your life is worth to your creator? Why or why not?

3. Did this chapter impact any of your previously held thoughts or beliefs? How or why?

Chapter 1. Created to Reflect
Dialogue guide

Reflection questions

Consider again:

> "You and I are valuable. Not because of anything we have accomplished or because of a particular skill or talent that we might possess, but because of Who created us and the purpose we were created to accomplish. We are masterpieces created by the greatest Artist of all time and put on display for the purpose of reflecting His image, majesty, wisdom, and character for all to see" (27).

4. What is your reaction to the paragraph above? Do you think it is accurate? Why or why not?

5. Where are some places you have attempted to find value in your life? What has been your experience with those attempts? How have those attempts worked for you? How have they worked against you? Explain your answer.

6. Would you say that your life is currently reflecting its intended purpose and design? Explain your answer.

Chapter 2. Searching for Significance
Dialogue guide

Excerpts from the reading

"God's design for our lives has careened off-course into a reflection of something less than His ideal. "

"Rather than embracing and resting in our divine design—to reflect the image and wisdom of our Creator through our lives—we are discontent with our intended purpose. We question our Creator's motives and His design for our lives...

...We are plagued with questions like, "Why them and not me?" and "What if God doesn't want me to be happy?" If we are honest with ourselves, we will see that our actions are often motivated by a craving for happiness and fulfillment. Entire areas of our lives revolve around pursuits which are attempts to validate our own existence."

"The pursuit of any goal—no matter how noble or desirable—other than the goal we were designed to accomplish, is a pursuit that will end in meaninglessness."

"If God's purpose for our lives is to reflect and display His own image, then it does not matter how noble or gratifying our priorities may be. They are attempts to place our wills above God's will."

Reflection questions

1. What ideas or images stood out to you in this chapter?

2. What was refreshing? Why?

3. What was frustrating? Why?

Chapter 2. Searching for Significance
Dialogue guide

Reflection questions

4. Take a moment and reflect on your life. Where are some areas in which you have sought validation in the past?

5. Write your response to the following quote. Do you agree or disagree with the quote? Explain your answer.

> "Every time we trade one false pursuit for validation for another false pursuit, we face the insanity of repeating the same process while expecting different results. One of the key quotes to this chapter is:
>
> "'The pursuit of any goal—no matter how noble or desirable—other than the goal we were designed to accomplish is a pursuit that will end in meaninglessness'" (44).

Chapter 3. Something Happened in the Garden
Dialogue guide

Excerpts from the reading

"The first battle of wills took place in the Garden of Eden and is recorded in the book of Genesis."

"This story relates an internal battle over whether Adam and Eve would choose to trust God and live in harmony with His design for their lives—or whether they would choose to make their own paths in defiance of God's instructions and clearly expressed will."

"This raises an obvious question: how could light, or a day and night, have existed before the creation of a sun, moon, and stars?"

"Jesus was not only with God in the beginning, but He was God from the beginning."

"Jesus was responsible for all of creation."

"Jesus brought light to the world prior to the creation of the sun."

"Why would God not create the sun until the fourth day?"

"What are the implications of what happened in the Garden of Eden between Adam, Eve, and God?"

"Does God really have your best interests at heart?"

"How does the choice to replace God's will with our own impact His overall design for our lives?"

"Just like Adam and Eve, we question God's intentions toward us. We exchange the light of His plan and design for the darkness of our own desires."

Reflection questions

1. God separated light from darkness before creating the sun, moon, and stars. Had you ever considered the practical question of light and darkness as they pertain to the historical account of creation? Why do you think God did this? What is your response to the significance of the biblical account?

2. Describe your thoughts about the biblical description of Jesus as the light of the world.

Chapter 3. Something Happened in the Garden
Dialogue guide

Reflection questions

3. Take a few quiet moments and consider the implications of what it would be like to truly reflect the light of Christ with your life. Write your thoughts.

4. What are some places or areas in your life that you have traded the light of Jesus for the light of other gods?

5. What are your thoughts concerning the intentions or motives of God toward you? What experiences have you had that have directed you to arrive at your conclusions?

6. What are some places you find yourself having placed your own will above God's will or direction in your life? What has been the result?

Chapter 4. Good Intentions and Dirty Rags
Dialogue guide

Excerpts from the reading

"Once we cross that line and begin to question God's motives toward us, it is relatively easy to begin asking questions like: 'Why should I submit to God's will if I don't know if I trust His intentions toward me? Why shouldn't I sit on the throne of my own life and live by my own rules—especially since my way of living seems more pleasurable and desirable?'"

"For others, it has meant following selfish desires that have resulted in broken relationships, ruined finances, or lost opportunities. Instead of finding joy and freedom, we become enslaved by the very things we thought would bring us life. And we experience the pain of watching dreams, careers, or even relationships die as a result of our pursuit of the very things we thought would bring us freedom."

"The ramifications of Adam and Eve's decision to respond to God by sitting on the thrones of their own lives, choosing to live in rebellion against God's will, still impact our lives every day."

"Yet, beneath our brokenness and regret, each of us still bear the image of the God who we were created to reflect, in spite of His full reflection being marred and muddied by our rebellious attempts to place our will over His. And yet, there are moments in our mud-covered lives where His purpose and design still shine through, allowing us to catch glimpses of His character, glory, and purpose. These moments emphasize the ironic truth that sinful and messed-up people are still capable of profound kindness, goodness, and courage."

"The truth beneath our acts of righteousness is that we can never fully clean our reflections while using a dirty rag."

"We must have a clear model of perfection to give direction to our lives and to give us an accurate measurement to determine where we are in the process of growth."

Reflection questions

1. In your life, what are some areas in which you can relate to having been on the receiving end of the bad intentions of others?

2. Have you ever considered how some of these negative experiences may have impacted your trust in God's intentions for your life?

3. Where have some of your own intentions led you?

Chapter 4. Good Intentions and Dirty Rags
Dialogue guide

Reflection questions

4. What are some areas in which you can see the consequences of personal sin impacting your life?

5. What is your reaction to the concept of your actions being like filthy rags?

6. In which areas do you find yourself attempting to use filthy rags to remove the effects of sin in your life?

7. After reading this chapter, what are your thoughts about your attempts?

Chapter 5. A Perfect Reflection
Dialogue guide

Excerpts from the reading

"Our sinfulness does not nullify our calling to reflect the image and glory of God in every area of our lives."

"Unless God chooses to open His hand and reveal Himself to us, we not only have no way of knowing what He is like, but we have no idea whether or not our ideas are even close."

"Does God really expect me to be a perfect reflection, or is He just suggesting that as a 'best case scenario?'"

"Our culture's depiction of Jesus is less a reflection of the real Son of God and more an example of the famous saying credited to the philosopher Voltaire: 'God created man in His own image and then we returned the favor.'"

"Is God's intention that we spend our lives memorizing every obscure biblical rule or law in order to walk a spiritual tightrope—motivated by our fear of falling off?"

Reflection questions

1. In your words, how does our culture portray Jesus?

2. How might the image of Jesus that is projected by our culture impact your perspective of Him?

3. Does your perspective of Jesus lean more toward a view of Him inviting you to memorize rules, or more toward the "smile more, swear less" Jesus? Why?

4. Did this chapter challenge that view of Jesus in your mind? Explain your response.

Notes page

101

Chapter 6. Redemption by Blood
Dialogue Guide

Excerpts from the reading

"In order for the people of God to re-embrace their divine calling and re-align themselves to His divine design for their lives, they need to be cleansed."

"1. Why did Jesus have to die?

2. How are the Old and New Testament connected?

3. What's the deal with the killing of animals in the Old Testament, and how are they connected to Christ's death on the cross?"

"Shame connotes feelings of unworthiness, regret, separation, and disgrace."

"Ever since Adam and Eve's first disobedience introduced sin and death into the world, God, in His love, mercy, and forbearance, offered a series of substitutions that gave His people a way to be reconciled with Himself."

"In God's divine plan, Christ's substitution is the only solution for "muddied mirrors" to become perfected reflections. Our journey must begin by accepting the gift of justification offered through the lavish grace that He pours out for us through the atoning work of Jesus Christ."

Reflection questions

1. Has there been a time in your life when you tried hiding from God, as Adam and Eve did? What were the results?

2. What are your thoughts on how God designed the sacrificial system to lead us to understand the concept of Jesus as our ultimate sacrifice?

3. How does understanding the system of sacrifices change your perspective of God? How does it change your perspective of Jesus?

Chapter 6. Redemption by Blood
Dialogue guide

Reflection questions

4. Are there any ways in which Jesus becomes more of a hero in your mind after reading this chapter? Explain.

5. If you were to examine yourself right now, would you say you are trying to create your own covering for your sin? Or have you accepted Christ's atonement covering? Explain your answer.

Chapter 7. The Fullness of Christ
Dialogue guide

Excerpts from the reading

"How do we live in a way that accurately reflects God and His glory in every area of life?"

"Rather than seeking His own comfort or glory, Jesus humbled Himself to the will of the Father. Jesus is a perfect reflection of God's love."

"Jesus practiced what He preached. He modeled a life that reflected the will of the Father and demonstrated God's design by submitting His life to the will of the Father."

"The bottom line is that we are to imitate God, just as Christ did, and we are to become mature, which is defined as reflecting the 'whole measure of the fullness of Christ.'"

"When we live in our purpose to reflect Jesus and when we follow His example to glorify God by submitting our lives to His will, we return to our original design and give eternal meaning to our temporary lives."

"Receiving Christ's gift of forgiveness is just the beginning. Following Him and learning to trust and reflect Him in every area of your life will equip you with the understanding and confidence that will deepen the meaning of your life in every way."

Reflection questions

1. What ideas or images stood out to you in this chapter?

2. What was refreshing? Why?

3. What was frustrating? Why?

How does the fullness of Christ apply to my everyday life?

Integrated =

Integrity =

Disintegrated =

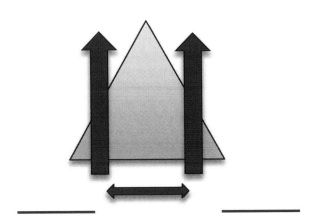

_____   _____

_____

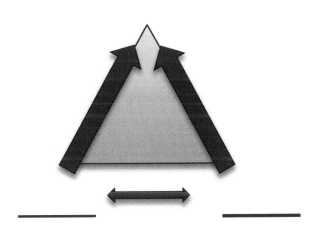

_____   _____

_____

How does the fullness of Christ apply to my everyday life?

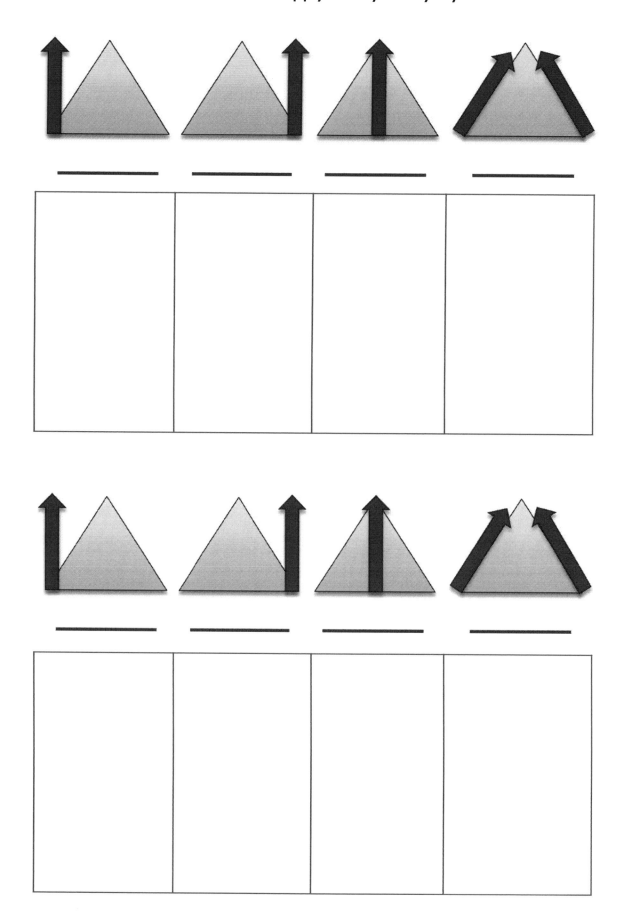

How does the fullness of Christ apply to my everyday life?

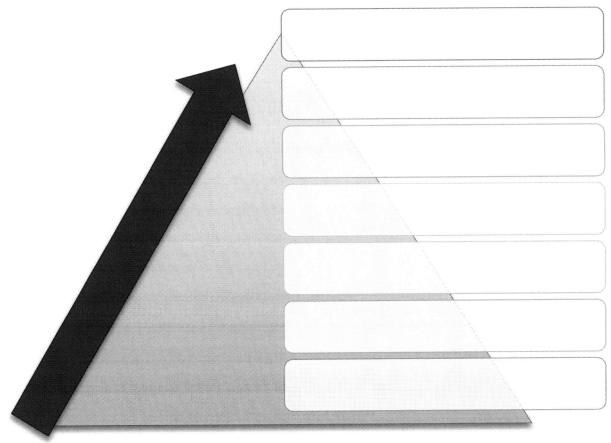

Material   **Spiritual**

1.

2.

3.

4.

5.

6.

7.

Notes and dialogue

Self-assessment and reflection paper

You are responsible for writing a one-page paper using the guidelines for a one-page paper in Bible class. Your paper will be graded on the following, based on the proficiency rubric:

Interaction with the questions (did you answer each of the questions?)
Interaction with the material (did you interact with the concepts learned in class?)
Higher level thinking (does your paper demonstrate a basic repetition of the material, or are you able to demonstrate understanding and articulate application?)

Part I. What have I learned? (Graded)

(60%) Answer the question: "What have I learned?"

- Use your notes. What are two things that are the most meaningful, intriguing, or challenging to you from these first three units?

- Your response can include new concepts, new skills, or new understandings.

- Explain your answer while demonstrating an academic understanding of the two areas you chose, as well as a personal explanation for why you chose what you did.

(30%) Finish and explain the following statement: "One of the biggest learning concepts or skills that was a challenge for me during the first three units was _____."

- Explain your answer.

- Demonstrate interaction with the material.

- If it was a learning challenge, how have you addressed the challenge?

- What will your next steps be? (Either to continue to overcome the challenge, or to apply and grow in what you are learning)

- Make sure your response demonstrates understanding and application of the content or skill development.

Part II. Life application

Look back at what you have learned over this first quarter and answer the following two questions:

- How was my faith challenged, or how did my faith grow, as a result of this quarter?

- (10%) What are two goals for improvement in the next quarter?

Proficiency scale

Standard	Element not present for assessment	Does not meet standard	Meets standard at basic level	Proficient in standard
	1	2	3	4
[CCSS.ELA-Literacy.W.9-10.1a] Introduce precise claim(s), distinguish the claim(s) from alternate or opposing claims, and create an organization that establishes clear relationships among claim(s), counterclaims, reasons, and evidence. ***Introduction: Minimum four sentences.***	Element not present.	Demonstrates little, if any, knowledge or understanding of the essential questions, concepts, or definitions explicitly taught in class.	Demonstrates basic knowledge or understanding of material explicitly taught in class.	Demonstrates knowledge or understanding of essential questions, concepts, and definitions at a higher level of interaction beyond what was explicitly taught in class.
[CCSS.ELA-Literacy.W.9-10.1b] Develop claim(s) and counterclaims fairly, supplying evidence for each while pointing out the strengths and limitations of both in a manner that anticipates the audience's knowledge level and concerns. ***What are two things that are the most meaningful to you from these first three units? (Use your notes. Your response can include new concepts, new skills, or new understandings.)***	Element not present.	Demonstrates little, if any, knowledge or understanding of the essential questions, concepts, or definitions explicitly taught in class.	Demonstrates basic knowledge or understanding of material explicitly taught in class.	Cites strong and thorough evidence to support analysis of what was explicitly taught in class and inferences drawn where class left matters uncertain.
[CCSS.ELA-Literacy.W.9-10.1c] Use words, phrases, and clauses to link the major sections of the text, create cohesion, and clarify the relationships between claim(s) and reasons, between reasons and evidence, and between claim(s) and counterclaims. ***Explain your answers while demonstrating an academic understanding of the two areas you chose, as well as a personal explanation for why you chose what you did.***	Element not present.	Demonstrates little, if any, knowledge or understanding of the essential questions, concepts, or definitions explicitly taught in class.	Demonstrates basic knowledge or understanding of two academic concepts, with little to no evidence of personal interaction with the material.	Demonstrates knowledge or understanding of how two concepts or skills relate or are opposed, while also providing evidence for personal conclusions.
[CCSS.ELA-Literacy.W.9-10.1d] Establish and maintain a formal style and objective tone while attending to the norms and conventions of the discipline in which [you] are writing. ***One of the biggest learning concepts or skills that was a challenge for me during the first three units was _____.***	Element not present.	Demonstrates little, if any, knowledge or understanding of the essential questions, concepts, or definitions explicitly taught in class.	Demonstrates knowledge or understanding of how a concept or skill presented a challenge.	Demonstrates Level 3 knowledge and understanding and demonstrates higher level critical thinking regarding how a Christ-centered theist views and would interact with the challenge.
[CCSS.ELA-Literacy.W.9-10.1e] Provide a concluding statement or section that follows from and supports the argument presented. ***Personal reflection: Explain how you will overcome the challenge and describe your next steps in personal application.***	Element not present.	Demonstrates little, if any, knowledge or understanding of the essential questions, concepts, or definitions explicitly taught in class.	Demonstrates basic knowledge or understanding of material explicitly taught in class and provides personal reflection, while also demonstrating a basic strategy for personal application.	Demonstrates Level 3 knowledge and understanding and includes material pulled from additional paragraphs to provide a comprehensive conclusion.

Learning objectives in the application section of the paper will be based on the following scale of proficiency.

0	1	2
Not attempted.	Student demonstrates a generic or simplistic application. Sentences or thoughts are not complete, or they do not meet the minimum of four sentences for a complete paragraph. Student demonstrates basic (if any) interaction with the material in a personal way. Thoughts are generic in nature.	Evidence is given that the student interacted with the significance of their beliefs in a meaningful way. References are made to the student's beliefs and how those beliefs impact his or her life. Interaction demonstrates higher level thought, critical thinking, and personal reflection. Thoughts are complete and demonstrate an interaction with the material in paragraphs that are a minimum of four sentences.

Grade:

Your paper will be typed or written in pen. It will consist of a minimum of four paragraphs, with a minimum of four sentences in each paragraph (following the one-page paper outline for Bible class). 60% of your grade will be your demonstration of what you have learned. 30% of your grade will be your interaction and reflection on your learning challenge. 10% of your grade will be your interaction with your two personal learning goals for this next quarter.

Specific measured standards for this paper include:

- [CCSS.ELA-Literacy.W.9-10.1] Write arguments to support claims in an analysis of substantive topics or texts, using valid reasoning and relevant and sufficient evidence.

- [CCSS.ELA-Literacy.W.9-10.1a] Introduce precise claim(s), distinguish the claim(s) from alternate or opposing claims, and create an organization that establishes clear relationships among claim(s), counterclaims, reasons, and evidence.

- [CCSS.ELA-Literacy.W.9-10.1b] Develop claim(s) and counterclaims fairly, supplying evidence for each while pointing out the strengths and limitations of both in a manner that anticipates the audience's knowledge level and concerns.

- [CCSS.ELA-Literacy.W.9-10.1c] Use words, phrases, and clauses to link the major sections of the text, create cohesion, and clarify the relationships between claim(s) and reasons, between reasons and evidence, and between claim(s) and counterclaims.

- [CCSS.ELA-Literacy.W.9-10.1d] Establish and maintain a formal style and objective tone while attending to the norms and conventions of the discipline in which [you] are writing.

- [CCSS.ELA-Literacy.W.9-10.1e] Provide a concluding statement or section that follows from and supports the argument presented.

How will I be graded?
Socratic rubric

Standard	Element not present for assessment	Does not meet standard	Meets standard at basic level	Above average in standard	Proficient in standard
	1	2	3	4	5
Conduct	Arrives unprepared without notes, pencil/pen, or perhaps even without the text.	Displays little respect for the learning process. Argumentative or apathetic. Takes advantage of minor distractions. Uses inappropriate language. Speaks to individuals rather than ideas. Arrives unprepared without notes, pencil/pen, or perhaps even without the text.	Participates and expresses a belief that his/her ideas are important in understanding the text. May make insightful comments, but does not contribute to the progress of the conversation.	Generally shows composure, but may display impatience with contradictory or confusing ideas. Comments, but does not necessarily encourage others to participate.	Demonstrates respect for the learning process. Has patience with different opinions and complexity of ideas. Shows initiative by asking others for clarification. Brings others into the conversation. Moves the conversation forward. Speaks to all of the participants. Avoids talking too much.
Speaking and reasoning	Arrives unprepared without notes, pencil/pen, or perhaps even without the text.	Extremely reluctant to participate even when called upon. Comments are illogical and meaningless. May mumble or express incomplete ideas. Little or no account taken of previous comments or important ideas in the text.	Responds to questions but may have to be called upon by others. Has read the text but has not put much effort into preparing questions and ideas for the seminar. Comments take details into account but may not flow logically in conversation.	Responds to questions voluntarily. Comments show an appreciation for the text. Comments are logical, but not connected to other speakers. Ideas are interesting enough that others respond.	Understands questions asked before answering them. Cites evidence from text. Expresses thoughts in complete sentences. Moves conversation forward. Makes connections between ideas.
Listening	Arrives unprepared without notes, pencil/pen, or perhaps even without the text.	Appears uninvolved in the seminar. Comments display complete misinterpretation of questions or comments of other participants.	Appears to find some ideas unimportant while responding to others. May require questions or confusions to be repeated due to inattention. Takes few notes during the seminar in response to ideas and comments.	Generally pays attention and responds thoughtfully to ideas and questions of other participants and the leader. Absorption in own ideas may distract the participant from the ideas of others.	Pays attention to details. Writes down questions. Responses take into account all participants. Demonstrates that he/she has kept up. Points out faulty logic respectfully. Overcomes distractions.
Critical reading	Arrives unprepared without notes, pencil/pen, or perhaps even without the text.	Student is unprepared for the seminar. Important words, phrases, and/or ideas in the text are unfamiliar. No notes or questions are marked in the text. No attempt made to get help with difficult material.	Appears to have read or skimmed the text, but has not marked the text or made meaningful notes or questions. Little evidence of serious reflection prior to the seminar.	Has read the text and comes with some ideas from it, but these may not be written out in advance. Occasionally references terms and page numbers.	Thoroughly familiar with the text. Has notations and questions in the margins (when applicable). Key words, phrases, and ideas are highlighted. Possible contradictions are identified. Uses terms and page numbers where appropriate.

Is the Bible true?

Foundations of Faith

INVITED TO BELIEVE

Unit Essential Questions

1. Is the Bible trustworthy?

2. Is the Bible God's revealed truth?

Unit Learning Objectives

A. To identify and examine reasonable evidence regarding the Bible as the revealed Word of God to see if what we have today is reliable

B. To identify and examine accusations and attacks against the Bible as the reliable and authoritative Word of God, and from a personal and apologetic position

Unit Learning Assessments

1. Formative quiz I

2. Formative quiz II

3. Summative unit exam

Essential Questions

1. Is the Bible worthy of our trust?

2. Where did the Bible come from, and what makes it a unique book?

3. Can we trust what was originally written?

4. What role did the scribes play in reliability?

5. The Shema project

6. Can we trust that we have the right books?

7. Are modern translations trustworthy and accurate?

8. Does the Bible have errors?

9. Is the Bible historically and geographically trustworthy?

10. How does archeology help us trust the reliability of the Bible?

11. Archeology project

12. Can we trust the prophecy in the Bible?

13. Why do I choose to believe the Bible?

14. Review: What have I learned?

15. Assessment: How will I demonstrate what I have learned?

16. Assessment review: What do I still need to learn?

Review

We began with the question "What is faith?" and examined the differences between authentic, reasonable faith and fantasy.

Second, we progressed with the question "What is real?" by examining the two core components of reality and the five possible foundational systems of trust and belief through the lens of the seven questions.

Then we asked the question "What is true?" and defined truth as a person and not as an object that can be viewed subjectively. We examined the law of noncontradiction in light of the implications of each foundational worldview's response to relativism and pluralism.

In the last unit, we took a closer look at what Christ-centered theists believe and how Christ-centered theists respond to each of the seven foundational questions. Students also learned to critically examine beliefs through a series of community Socratic dialogues.

In this unit, we will examine the Bible to discover whether it is reasonable to believe it is the written revelation of God. We will also ask, "Is it trustworthy and reasonable to place our faith in the Bible as the accurate, authentic, and inerrant revelation of God?"

Application

Question: A friend finds out you go to a Christian school and asks you to provide reasons that Christians believe the Bible is actually the authentic, trustworthy revelation of God to man—not just another book by men about God. What are the top five reasons you would give to your friend? Explain your answers.

1.

2.

3.

4.

5.

Is the Bible worthy of our trust?

Learning objective: The original attack on the relationship between man and God occurred when our mutual enemy began to plant seeds of doubt regarding the reliability and trustworthiness of God's Word, as well as our ability to understand it.

Question 1: Have you ever doubted your ability to understand the Bible? Explain your answer.

Question 2: What was the source of the doubt? How has it impacted your view of and/or interaction with the Bible?

Read Genesis 3:1-7 and then answer the following questions.

1. Define crafty.

2. What are the implications of the word "crafty"?

3. What are the implications of the word "calculating"?

4. What was the long-term goal that the serpent was determined to accomplish with his question?

5. Read Genesis 3:1 and then write out the question asked by the serpent.

6. Read the verses below that actually contain God's instructions. In what way did the serpent twist God's words in his question to Adam and Eve?

   Genesis1:29

   Genesis1:30

   Genesis 2:16-17

Is the Bible worthy of our trust?

Questions continued

7. What is the difference between what the serpent accused God of saying and what God actually said?

8. What are the implications of the differences between the serpent's words and what God actually said?

Read Genesis 3:2-3 and then explain Eve's response in your own words.

1. What is the difference between what God actually said and the words Eve attributed to God? In what way did she add or subtract from God's words?

2. What is the implication of the difference between what God said and what Eve said He did?

Read Genesis 3:3-5 and then answer the following questions.

1. What is true about what was said? What is false about what was said? What is the implication of the difference?

2. List the three things that Eve considered about the fruit in the process of choosing to eat it.

3. Cross-reference the concepts of temptation and desire found in Genesis 3 with James 1:14-16. Then highlight or underline some of the similarities and differences between the two passages in your Bible. Write what stands out to you in the space below.

Is the Bible worthy of our trust?

It is easy to sometimes approach the Bible with one foot in and one foot out. We wonder whether it is truly God's Word and whether we can trust what it says. If it is truly God's Word, and if it is trustworthy, then what should our approach to it be?

The crafty process the serpent used with Adam and Eve is still working to invite us to question the Word of God: "Did God really say…?"

Our enemy still uses the same tactics today as he did with Adam and Eve.

He plays on our ignorance for the purpose of planting doubt. He wants us to question and mistrust the accuracy of what is written, how relevant it is to our lives, and whether or not God's intentions toward us have our best interests in mind.

We fall into trouble when we, like Eve, misquote and misapply God's Word, either because we are ignorant or because we intentionally desire to rebel against it. We also fall into trouble when we relate to God's Word without having confidence in whether or not it is completely trustworthy.

The Bible says God has given us everything we need to have knowledge of Him and to live a life of godliness, but if we put words in His mouth or doubt His love and intentions toward us, then we will miss the opportunity to know and apply the truth of God's Word to our lives.

> "His divine power has given us everything we need for a godly life through our knowledge of him who called us by his own glory and goodness."
> - 2 Peter 1:3, NIV

- Examine 2 Timothy 3:1-2 and highlight or underline it in your Bible. In what ways might it be comforting to know that Paul, under the inspiration of the Holy Spirit, told Timothy what to expect?

- Read 2 Timothy 3:14-17 and list some personal applications from these instructions to Timothy that you can apply to your own life.

The next couple of lessons will address the enemy's attacks on the reliability of the Word of God, by inviting us to ask difficult questions and to examine the evidence for ourselves.

- Is the Bible reliable and accurate?

- Is what we have what was written, or was it changed?

- Was the original written material trustworthy?

Where did the Bible come from?
Video notes

Write a response that addresses the following three questions and turn it in during the next class.

1. What is one thing you learned?

2. What is your reaction to the stories of those who gave their lives so you could have access to the Bible?

3. Did this video challenge the way you view the Bible? Explain your response.

- Based on what you heard in the video, summarize who wrote the Bible.

- Based on what you heard in the video, can we trust what was originally written? Why or why not?

- Based on what you heard in the video, is the Bible reliable and accurate? Why or why not?

What makes the Bible a unique book?

"The Bible was written over a period of 1,500 years in various places stretching all the way from Babylon to Rome. The human authors included over 40 different people from various stations in life: kings, peasants, poets, herdsman, fishermen, scientists, farmers, priests, pastors, tentmakers, and governors … yet it speaks with agreement and reliability … No PERSON could have possibly conceived or written such a work." - Josh McDowell

- Why does this matter?

Comparing the Bible against other books

The Bible is translated from over 24,000 copies of the New Testament alone, with millions of people having seen some of those copies. The copies have been translated by thousands of scholars.	The Book of Mormon is translated from a supposed single original that was claimed to have been seen and translated by one man: Joseph Smith (who was not an expert in languages and was convicted of occult activity). That original was "taken back." There are no copies of that original.
The Bible was written by more than 40 different authors, spanning over 50 generations and three continents. It speaks with agreement on all matters of faith and doctrine.	The Qur'an consists of the writings and record of one man, Muhammad, in one place at one point in history. It differs at many points with the Old and New Testament accounts of history.

Can we trust what was originally written?

A. Examine the eyewitness accounts

- Luke 1:1-4

- Acts 1:15-22

- Acts 2:29-33

- 1 Corinthians 15:3-7

- 1 John 1

B. What does it mean when we say the Bible is inerrant?

C. Can we trust that we have what was originally written?

Author	Date written	Earliest copy	Difference	Number of copies
Caesar (Gallic Wars)	100-44 B.C.	A.D. 900		
Plato	400 B.C.	A.D. 900		
Pliny the Younger	A.D. 61-113	A.D. 900		
Aristotle	384-322 B.C.	A.D. 1100		
Homer	900 B.C.	A.D. 400		
New Testament	A.D. 50-90	Before A.D. 100 (Fragments of Mark, Matthew)		

What role do the scribes play in reliability?

Masoretic Copying Rules

- Each scroll must contain a specified number of columns, all equal through the whole book.

- The length of each column must not be less than 48 lines or more than 60 lines.

- Each column's breadth must be exactly 30 letters.

- The copyist must use a specially prepared black ink.

- The copyist must not copy from memory.

- The space between every consonant must be the size of a thread.

- The copyist must sit in full Jewish dress.

- The copyist must use a fresh quill to pen the sacred name of God.

- The copyist could only copy letter by letter, not word by word.

- The copyist counted the number of times each letter of the alphabet occurred in each book, and if it came out wrong, the entire scroll was thrown away.

- The copyist knew the middle letter of the Pentateuch and the middle letter of the entire Old Testament. After copying a scroll, the copyist counted. If it did not match, the entire scroll was thrown away.

What role did the scribes play in reliability?

The Dead Sea Scrolls are one of the most famous archaeological discoveries. Every book in the Old Testament is found in these scrolls. Prior to their discovery, some of the earliest biblical manuscripts dated from A.D. 900 (almost 1000 years later). When compared, there were practically no differences.

Example: The Hittites

Video Homework:

A. Notes:

B. What is one thing you learned?

C. What is one question you still have?

The Shema project

Before the invention of the printing press, the responsibility of copying and preserving the Old Testament (Tanakh) writings fell on a group of Jewish scribes. They so revered and honored the Word of God that they developed an extensive set of rules to ensure they copied it accurately. The meticulous process of hand-copying a scroll took over 2000 hours on average. All that work would immediately be disqualified if:

- A single letter was added
- A single letter was deleted
- The scribe who wrote it was not pious
- The materials used did not conform to the strict specifications
- The scribe wrote even one letter from memory, rather than copying it exactly
- The scribe did not pronounce every word out loud before he wrote it
- Any of the letters were touching one another
- There was not a sufficient white space between words
- A single letter was smeared or looked like another letter
- Any of the line lengths, paragraphs, or breakup of the text was altered in any way

These are just a few of the hundreds of rules that were created to ensure the accurate copying of the Tanakh.

Today you are going to experience a taste of the life of a scribe.

1. A scribe began his day by ceremonially cleaning himself in preparation for copying Scripture. (Using hand sanitizer, clean your hands so you can prepare to copy Scripture.)
2. Every day, a scribe would mix exactly enough ink for only that day. They never kept leftover ink for the next day. (Get two pens.)
3. Then they would take out the scroll and prepare it by creating a grid on the scroll. This process would help them ensure that letters did not touch, lines were straight, and they could copy it exactly as it appeared on the other scroll. (Take out a piece of paper.)
4. Every time the word "Yahweh" (the proper name for God) appeared, the scribe would put down his pen, go and rewash himself, then write the name of God using a different pen. (Go rewash your hands, sit back down, and write the word "Yahweh" with a different pen.)
5. The scribe would continue to follow this system the entire time he wrote.
6. If at any point he made a mistake, the scroll would be buried in the ground so that no one would mistakenly use it. (If at any point you break any of the rules above, you must take your paper, discard the entire thing, and start over.)

Once the scroll was completed, a different scribe would go through a system of guidelines to check the accuracy of the scroll.

1. The scribe would count every letter on each page to see if the letter count was the same as the original. If it was not, the scroll would be discarded.
2. He would count how many times each letter was used on the scroll. If it was not accurate, the scroll would be discarded.
3. He would count to find the middle letter on each page and compare it to the original. If it was not accurate, the scroll would be discarded.
4. He would look to see if there were any letters touching. If there were, the scroll would be discarded.
5. He would check to see if there were any words touching. If there were, the scroll would be discarded.
6. He would also check to see if there were any ink blots or smudges. If there were, the scroll would be discarded.

The Shema project

שְׁמַע יִשְׂרָאֵל יְהוָה אֱלֹהֵינוּ יְהוָה אֶחָד
וְאָהַבְתָּ אֵת יְהוָה אֱלֹהֶיךָ בְּכָל־
לְבָבְךָ וּבְכָל־נַפְשְׁךָ וּבְכָל־מְאֹדֶךָ :

"Hear, O Israel! The LORD is our God, the LORD is one! You shall love the LORD your God with all your heart and with all your soul and with all your might."

Deuteronomy 6:4-5

What is textual criticism?

Can we trust that we have the right books?

What three things were considered when it came to deciding what books were to be included in the New Testament canon?

1.

2.

3.

Paul quotes from Deuteronomy 25:4 (the Old Testament) and Luke 10:7 (the New Testament), calling them both Scripture. Luke's Gospel was written in A.D. 60 and the Book of 1 Timothy was written in A.D. 63. This means that the Gospel of Luke was being recognized as Holy Scripture within three years of its writing.

> "He said to them, 'This is what I told you while I was still with you: Everything must be fulfilled that is written about me in the Law of Moses, the Prophets and the Psalms.'"
>
> - Luke 24:44, NIV

> "For Scripture says, 'Do not muzzle an ox while it is treading out the grain,' and 'The worker deserves his wages.'"
>
> - 1 Timothy 5:18, NIV

Why does this matter?

Can we trust that we have the right books?
What about the Apocrypha?

A. What about the Apocrypha?

Define Apocrypha:

- What are some of the arguments against the inclusion of the Apocrypha in the canon of Scripture?

    - Whatever Scriptures Christ used in the first century are the Scriptures we should use today.
    - The Scripture of the Palestinian Jews in the first century contained the same books as the current 39-book Protestant canon, as evidenced by the New Testament itself, Philo, Josephus, and the Talmud.
    - The New Testament never directly quotes from any apocryphal book as Scripture, using the common designation of "it is written."
    - The Apocrypha testifies that there was an absence of prophets during the time it was written:

    "Thus there was great distress in Israel, such as had not been since the time that prophets ceased to appear among them."

    -1 Maccabees 9:27, RSVCE

Reflection and dialogue

Do you find these arguments convincing? Why or why not?

If you were asked to defend the 66-book canon, what evidence would you choose to use?

Can we trust that we have the right books?
What about the Gnostic Gospels?

- ## What is Gnosticism?

  Gnosticism is the heretical belief that spirit is good and matter is evil.

  As a result, gnostics not only taught that they had "special knowledge" apart from Scripture, but that Jesus could not have physically been a real person because that would have made Him evil.

  The New Testament writers were very aware of the gnostics. In fact, there is much written in the New Testament to refute the heresy of Gnosticism. A few examples include:

  - 1 Corinthians

  - Galatians

  - 1 John

- ## What are some examples of Gnostic Gospels?

  A. Thomas

  B. Peter

  C. Judas

  D. Other

Can we trust that we have the right books?
What role did the confirmation of the church play in the process?

People often think that the New Testament books were chosen by a few people, but that is not true. A council recognized the books around A.D. 400, after the church had been using them for around 300 years. They were formally recognized in response to false teachers who were trying to introduce new books into the accepted canon. The word "canon" is a term describing a theological concept used to identify the collection of books called Scripture. The canon is now closed because God is no longer revealing Scripture through the writing of validated messengers. One reason is because soteriological history has been completed and recorded, so there is no longer a need for any Scriptures to be added to the canon. All major traditions of Christianity today believe that the canon is closed and not to be reopened.

Are modern translations trustworthy?

A. Why are there so many translations, and are they reliable?

Consider the following facts:

Modern translations vary in language.

- There are over 7,000 known languages in the world.

- The Bible was originally written in only three languages: Hebrew, Aramaic, and Greek.

- Without translations, people who speak other languages would not be able to have access to the Bible.

- Currently, Wycliffe Bible Translators say there are around 1,900 languages that are still waiting for a Bible in their language. Wycliffe's goal is to see the Bible translated into those remaining languages by 2025. (For more information, check out wycliffe.org)

Modern translations vary in purpose.

- Some, like the ESV or the NASB, were translated to get a word for word, literal translation.

- Others, like the NIV, were translated to get a thought for thought translation that reads more smoothly but may lose some of the exactness of the wording.

- Still others, like The Message or The Living Bible, were translated as a paraphrase translation. These may miss some of the specific nuances of individual words, but they were designed to help make the Bible more accessible.

Modern translations use the same reliable primary sources.

- There are several primary sources for modern-day Bible translations that are available for scholars to use.

- Codex Sinaiticus is one of the most important books in the world. It was handwritten more than 1,600 years ago. The manuscript contains the Bible in Greek and is the oldest complete copy of the New Testament

- The Dead Sea Scrolls (discovered in 1947) and the Septuagint (a Greek translation of the Hebrew Bible, written around 200-150 B.C.) have both validated a copy of the Hebrew Bible known as the Masoretic text, which dates back to the 10th or 11th century.

B. What are the differences in translation types?

Reflection

A friend tells you he has decided not to trust the reliability of the Bible because he heard modern translations are simply copies of a copy of a copy, much like the game of Telephone you may have played when you were younger. The message has changed over time, and that is why we have so many different modern translations. How would you respond?

What evidence would you use to give reasoned responses to the following questions?

1. Why do so many translations exist?

1. Are modern day translations simply copies of copies?

2. What are the sources for modern-day translations?

3. What are the differences in translation types and what are reliable translations to use?

Does the Bible have errors?
Do differing biblical texts contradict, collaborate with, or complement each other?

A. What do the words "inerrancy" and "infallibility" mean?

Inerrancy:

Infallibility:

B. What are some of the arguments for the inerrancy of Scripture?

Does the Bible have errors?

Does the Bible contain contradictions?

Defining the terms:

Collaborate:

Confirm:

Collusion:

Example I. The death of Saul

1 Samuel 31:4-6

2 Samuel 1:1-16

Explain your response.

Example II. The death of Judas

Matthew 27:5

Acts 1:18

Explain your response.

Examine the evidence

Example III. Errors in transcription

2 Samuel 10:18, NASB	1 Chronicles 19:18, NASB
"But the Arameans fled before Israel, and David killed 700 charioteers of the Arameans and 40,000 horsemen and struck down Shobach the commander of their army, and he died there."	"The Arameans fled before Israel, and David killed of the Arameans 7,000 charioteers and 40,000 foot soldiers, and put to death Shophach the commander of the army."

How is this explained?

Example IV. Phenomenological Language

Isaiah 13:10, NASB	Solution
"For the stars of heaven and their constellations will not flash forth their light; the sun will be dark when it rises and the moon will not shed its light."	An over-emphasis on scientific precision does not consider language that speaks from the perspective of the subject. For example, the U.S. Naval Almanac uses the language of "rising" and "setting" sun.

Example V. Poor understanding of genre

Proverbs 12:21, NET	Luke 16:19–22
"The righteous do not encounter any harm, but the wicked are filled with calamity."	In this parable, the unrighteous, rich man is without harm, while the righteous, poor man is experiencing calamity.

Understanding and application: a proverb is a general truth and does not apply to every situation. In application, a righteous man may experience temporal calamity in the present world while experiencing no harm in eternity.

Additional considerations

1.

2.

3.

4.

Notes:

Is the Bible historically and geographically trustworthy?

The Book of Acts is a model of historical accuracy. In it, Luke names 32 countries, 54 cities, and nine islands without error.

Luke begins his Gospel by informing the reader that it is a carefully researched account from eyewitnesses (Luke 1:1-4).

As Paul's personal physician, Luke would have had access to interviewing eyewitnesses through his direct and immediate contact with the disciples (Acts 15:4-7).

Why does this matter?

Old Testament geography

A. The Bible takes place during the real course of human history and within real _____.

- Understanding geographical context builds _____ .

    This is important to know because _____

- Understanding geographical context builds _____.

B. The major land areas can be identified by the major bodies of _____ that act as markers.

To position places on a map, think of the bodies of water as a clock with a center.

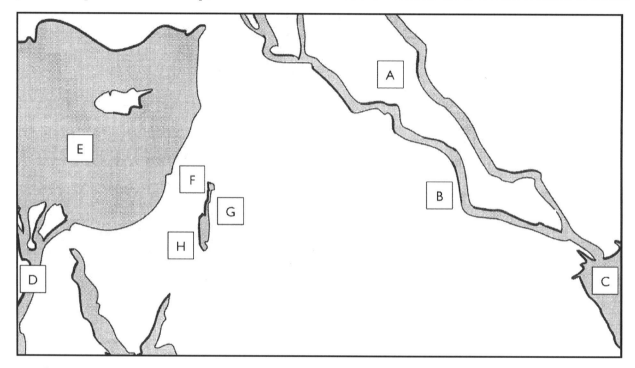

Start at the top right hand side of the map and work your way around clockwise.

    A. and B. The Tigris and Euphrates Rivers flow into

    C. The Persian Gulf

    D. The Nile River

    E. The Mediterranean Sea

At the center of the clock are three bodies of water.

    F. The Sea of Galilee

    G. The Jordan River

    H. The Dead Sea

Old Testament geography

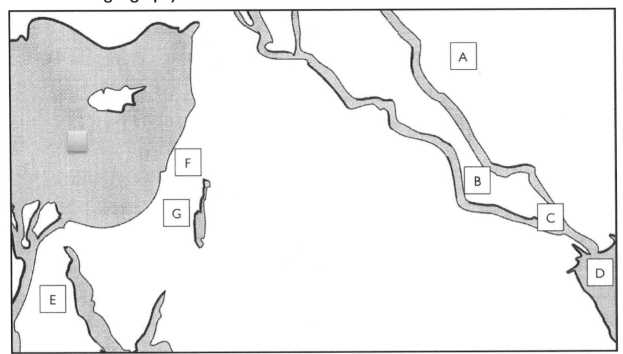

The major land areas of the Old Testament can be located using bodies of water as identifiers.

A. Assyria

B. Babylon

C. Eden*

D. Persia

E. Egypt

F. Israel

G. Jerusalem

New Testament geography in the Gospels

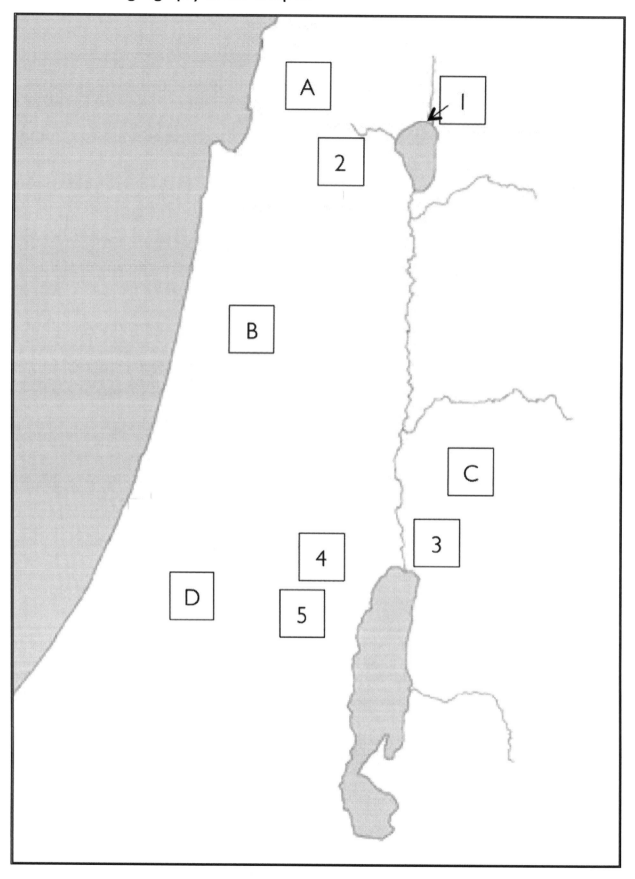

New Testament geography in the Gospels

The major cities and geographical areas of the Gospels are centrally located around the major bodies of water at the center of the Old Testament map.

A.   Galilee region

      1.   Capernaum

      2.   Nazareth

B.   Samaria region

C. Peraea region

    3. Bethany

D. Judaea region

    4. Jerusalem

    5. Bethlehem

New Testament geography

Throughout the historical book of Acts, as the gospel spreads to the rest of the world, the map begins to include more geographical locations.

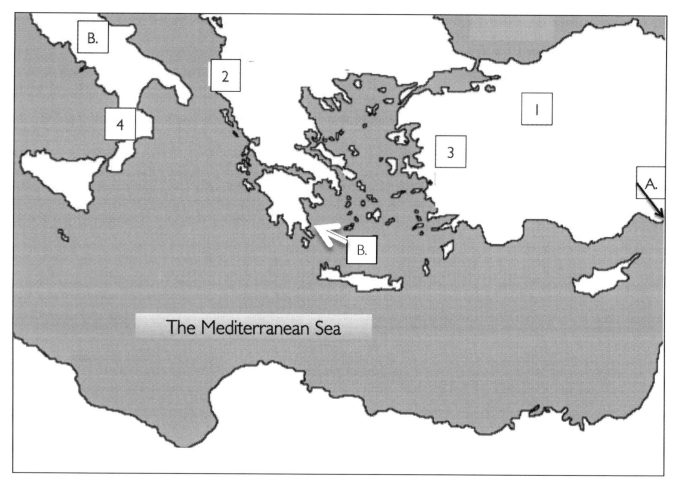

New Testament geography can be summarized by two central figures.

A. _____ Jerusalem, Judea, mission to the Jews

B. _____ Asia, Greece, Rome, mission to the Gentiles

New Testament geography

There are four primary countries that contain multiple cities.

The city of Antioch was the beginning for each of the three mission trips for the gospel.

1.   Paul's first missionary journey was to the country of _____.

2.   Paul's second missionary journey was to the country of _____.

3.   Paul's third missionary journey was to the country of _____.

4.   Paul was ultimately imprisoned and died in the country of _____.

How does archeology help us trust the reliability of the Bible?

Example A. How does archeology help us trust the reliability of the Bible? (Daniel)

Example B. How does archeology help us trust the reliability of the Bible? (Esther)

How does archeology help us trust the reliability of the Bible?

Example C. How does archeology help us trust the reliability of the Bible? (Hittites)

Archeology project

143

Can we trust the prophecy in the Bible?

Why does biblical prophecy matter?

Biblical prophecy is one of the ways we can build trust in the Bible and in its reliability.

Standing on the bank of the the Jordan River, looking over into the promised land of Israel, Moses prophesied about the future of the nation of Israel. Some of it would be fulfilled in the next 300 years, other parts over the period of the next 3,000 years. To be able to "foretell" exact events concerning individuals and nations thousands of years prior to those events happening is nothing short of a miracle.

The Bible is full of prophetic miracles: words spoken by humans through the inspiration of the Holy Spirit of God. There are three main categories of biblical prophecies that you will be examining for yourself in the next few class periods: prophecies concerning the nation of Israel, prophecies concerning other nations, and prophecies concerning the future Messiah.

Read and write in your own words. In Deuteronomy 18:21-22, what does Moses say about whether or not we know a message has been spoken by the Lord?

What does this mean? What are the implications of the words of Moses?

Examine for yourself.

A. What are some of the prophecies concerning the future of Israel?

B. What are some of the prophecies concerning the future of other nations?

C. What are some of the prophecies concerning the heritage of the Messiah?

- **Compare Genesis 9:26-27 with Luke 3:36**

    Out of the three sons of Noah, the Messiah would come through:

- **Genesis 12:2-3, 22:18**

    Out of the descendants of Shem, the Messiah would come through:

- **Genesis 21:12**

    Out of the two sons of Abraham, the Messiah would come through:

- **Genesis 35:10-12, Numbers 24:17**

    Out of the twelve sons of Jacob, the Messiah would come not through Joseph, but through:

- **Genesis 49:10, Psalm 78:67-68, Isaiah 11:1-2**

    Out of the descendants of Judah, all would be rejected except for the family of:

- **Jeremiah 23:5**

    Out of all of the sons of Jesse, all would be passed over except for:

Does Jesus meet the qualifications of being the Messiah?

Read Matthew 1 out loud and write a reflection on what you see regarding "the address" of Jesus, in comparison with the prophecies of the Old Testament.

In other words, the Messiah would be the one who was the son of

_____, the son of _____, the son of

_____, the son of _____, the son of

_____, the son of _____, the son of

_____.

D. Examine some of the prophecies about the birth of the Messiah for yourself

Compare Micah 5:2 with Matthew 2:1.

> "But you, Bethlehem Ephrathah, though you are small among the clans of Judah, out of you will come for me one who will be ruler over Israel, whose origins are from of old, from ancient times."
>
> Micah 5:2, NIV

> "After Jesus was born in Bethlehem in Judea, during the time of King Herod, Magi from the east came to Jerusalem."
>
> Matthew 2:1, NIV

God even sent several types of eyewitnesses to verify the fulfillment of the prophecy.

> "He [Herod] sent them [the Magi] to Bethlehem and said, 'Go and search carefully for the child. As soon as you find him, report to me, so that I too may go and worship him.'"
>
> Matthew 2:8, NIV

> "When Herod realized that he had been outwitted by the Magi, he was furious, and he gave orders to kill all the boys in Bethlehem and its vicinity who were two years old and under, in accordance with the time he had learned from the Magi."
>
> Matthew 2:16, NIV

> "When the angels had left them and gone into heaven, the shepherds said to one another, 'Let's go to Bethlehem and see this thing that has happened, which the Lord has told us about.'"
>
> Luke 2:15, NIV

E. Examine some of the prophecies about the life of the Messiah for yourself

Read the Old Testament prophecies about the life of Christ and then identify the New Testament fulfillment.

- What do Malachi 3:1 and Malachi 4:5 say?

- What does Isaiah 9:1 say?

Read the Old Testament prophecies about the life of Christ and then identify the New Testament fulfillment.

- Zechariah 9:9

- Haggai 2:7

- Malachi 3:1

- Isaiah 35:5-6

- Psalm 78:2

- Psalm 118:22

- Psalm 41:9

- Psalm 55:12-14

- Zechariah 11:12-13

F. Examine some of the prophecies about the death of the Messiah for yourself

Read the Old Testament prophecies about the death of Christ and then identify the New Testament fulfillment.

- Zechariah 13:7

- Psalm 35:11

- Psalm 38:13a

- Isaiah 53:7

- Psalm 22:17-18

- Isaiah 53:12

- Isaiah 53:5

Read the Old Testament prophecies about the death of Christ and then identify the New Testament fulfillment.

- Psalm 22:16

- Psalm 22:1

- Psalm 22:7-8

- Isaiah 53:9

Reflection: What are the odds?

Why do I choose to believe the Bible?
Notes

Review
What have I learned?

151

How will I demonstrate what I have learned?

You are responsible for writing a two-page paper answering the following questions using the material you learned in Unit Four. To complete this assignment, you should use your notes and the PowerPoint slides from class.

Question 1. Choose three pieces of evidence that a Christ-centered theist would use to confidently conclude that the Bible is the revealed Word of God and that what we have is reliable.

Question 2. How has this unit challenged or impacted your perception of the Bible's reliability and your personal approach to how you view it?

	4	**3**	**2**	**1**
Clarity 4 points	Student effectively uses language to demonstrate personal understanding of concepts drawn from the material taught in class.	Student uses language to demonstrate personal understanding of concepts drawn from the material taught in class, but some concepts lack clarity or are not thoroughly explained.	Student does not demonstrate personal understanding of concepts because writing lacks clarity and concepts are not explained.	Student fails to communicate concepts or personal understanding.
Accuracy 16 points	Student shares three pieces of evidence and a personal reflection from the material taught in class.	Student shares fewer than three pieces of evidence and/or does not share a personal reflection from the concepts learned through the material taught in class.	Student shares much fewer than three pieces of evidence and/or does not share a personal reflection from the concepts learned through the material taught in class.	Student fails to share anything significant from the concepts learned through class.
Precision 4 points	Student follows standard writing guidelines, and there are no grammatical or spelling errors.	Student follows standard writing guidelines, but there are 1-3 grammatical or spelling errors that become distracting.	Student follows standard writing guidelines, but there are 4-5 distracting grammatical or spelling errors.	Student does not follow standard writing guidelines, and grammatical errors distract from the meaning of the paper.

What do I trust?

Foundations of Faith

Unit Essential Questions

1. What have I learned?

2. What do I trust?

Unit Learning Objectives

A. To design and present a presentation that identifies and evaluates three critical concepts learned during this class

B. To demonstrate understanding and application of the class essential questions through a written exam

Unit Learning Assessments

1. Final exam

2. Final presentation

3. Combination

Final Assessment Options

	Option A. Exam	Option B. Presentation	Option C. Combination
1.	Review Unit 1	Assign presentations	Assign final assessments
2.	Review Unit 2	Student workday	Student workday
3.	Review Unit 3	Presentations	Presentations
4.	Review Unit 4	Presentations	Presentations
5.	Review Unit 5	Presentations	Presentations
6.	Self-assessments Cloud of Witnesses video	Self-assessments Cloud of Witnesses video	Review guide due Self-assessment
7.	Final exam		Final exam

Student Name
Class, Period
Date

How to write a one-page paper for Bible class

It is not enough to simply memorize Bible facts or acquire biblical knowledge. Students need to be given the opportunity to wrestle with important issues, develop personal beliefs, and articulate those beliefs in clear and convincing ways, in both written and oral forms. At our school, we value the ability to think critically and communicate clearly about theological truth. It is the belief of the Bible Department that Bible classes offer the opportunity to practice and develop these skills through the medium of one-page papers.

One-page papers are made up of a centered title and four critical paragraphs. The first part of the paper is referred to as the "hook" paragraph, and it is used to relate the topic to the audience. The second part of the paper is the "book" paragraph. The purpose of this paragraph is to clearly state the main concept of the paper. The third paragraph is the "look" paragraph, and it is where the author illustrates the main point they outlined in the second paragraph. The fourth or final section is called the "took" paragraph. It is in this final paragraph that the author outlines a personal application, lesson, or "takeaway" from the topic.

Each individual paragraph must also contain a few key elements. One of the key elements is that each paragraph needs a minimum of four sentences. Another key element is that each paragraph needs to include transition sentences and be double-spaced. The paper is also written using either 11- or 12-point Times New Roman or Arial font. Finally, while the paper itself will use APA guidelines, it is important to note that the paper must not be longer than one page in total length (Bible Reference 1:1).

There are three main things I need to learn through these papers. First, I will have critically examined my personal beliefs. Second, I will have learned how to communicate my beliefs in concise written form. Third and finally, I will have a collection of papers outlining my beliefs to use for personal reference in the future.

DUAL CREDIT FOR STUDENTS

Wheaton Press is excited to offer students the opportunity to receive dual credit for their Bible classes through a unique partnership with Colorado Christian University. Each Wheaton Press course has been recognized as the equivalent of a college-level class. As a result, Wheaton Press courses provide the opportunity for your students to receive dual credit.

Participating students will receive

- The opportunity to gain college credit during their normal course work at an affordable rate.

- College credits that are transferable to 90% of colleges and universities.*

About Colorado Christian University

- Colorado Christian University, a four-year Christian university located in Denver, Colorado, is fully accredited through the Higher Learning Commission of the North Central Association of Colleges and Schools.

- This means that credits are transferable to almost any school in the nation, including state universities and private colleges.

How students participate

When your students choose the dual-credit option they are able to earn three college credits for only $200 per class while they are taking their regular Bible Class.

Your students participate in the same assessments regardless of whether or not they participate. There is no extra work or assessments to receive the college credit in addition to the credit they will be receiving through your school.

This means that your students have the opportunity to enter college or university with up to 21 transferable college credits for only $1,400 over the course of four years.

Students pay the $200 course fee at the time of their registration at CCU. This course fee is paid directly to CCU and not to your school.

Students must earn a C or above to ensure that credit is valid at CCU or other colleges and universities.

Note: Individual colleges and universities determine if they accept credit from Colorado Christian University.

In a recent survey conducted by CCU, over 90% of schools accepted their dual credit enrollment — including all public and private Christian universities surveyed.

Generally, the schools who did not accept their dual credit did not accept any form of college credit earned in high school — even AP credit.

Learn more at WheatonPress.com/DualCredit